16-19 MATHEMATICS

Further mathematics revision

The School Mathematics Project

CAMBRIDGE
UNIVERSITY PRESS

Authors		
	Chris Belsom	Donal Monaghan
	John Buckeridge	Val Mullard
	Alison Coates	David Ogden
	Mike Dams	Steve Pegg
	Jean Evanson	Jeff Searle
	Graham Hacking	Chris Thompson
	Andy Hall	Richard Warren
	Paul Healey	Anne Williams
	Neil Hendry	Ken Williams
	Bill Langton	Thelma Wilson
	Roger Lugsdin	John Wohlers

Edited by   Stan Dolan and Ann Kitchen

Project Administrator   Ann White

Published by the Press Syndicate of the University of Cambridge
The Pitt Building, Trumpington Street, Cambridge CB2 1RP
40 West 20th Street, New York, NY 10011-4211, USA
10 Stamford Road, Oakleigh, Melbourne 3166, Australia

© Cambridge University Press 1995

First published 1995

Produced by 16–19 Mathematics, Southampton

Printed in Great Britain at the University Press, Cambridge

ISBN 0 521 49828 7 paperback

Contents

MATHEMATICAL STRUCTURE

A binary operation ∘

This is a rule which assigns to each ordered pair a, b of elements of a set S an element denoted by $a \circ b$.

Some possible binary operations include:

- ordinary +, x, –, ÷ on sets of numbers;
- modulo (or clock) arithmetic operations;
- the combination of functions under the 'function of a function' rule;
- the combination of geometrical transformations, 'b followed by a'.

Example: $S = \{1, 3, 5, 7\}$, operation 'x mod 8'.

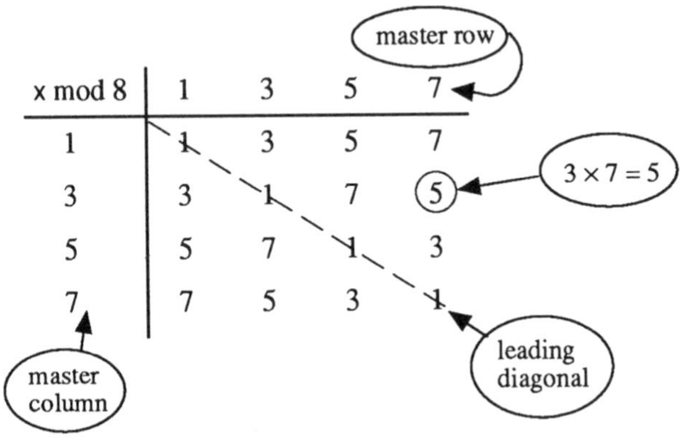

x mod 8	1	3	5	7
1	1	3	5	7
3	3	1	7	5
5	5	7	1	3
7	7	5	3	1

Properties

An operation ∘ on a set S **may** possess the following properties.

(a) **Identity element**: an element e in S such that $a \circ e = e \circ a = a$ for all a in S. (The identity leaves the master row and column unchanged.)

(b) **Associativity**: the operation ∘ is associative if $a \circ (b \circ c) = (a \circ b) \circ c$ for all a, b, c in S. (This can be time-consuming to prove but many standard operations such as the combination of geometrical transformations can be quoted as being associative.)

(c) **Commutativity**: operation ∘ is commutative if $a \circ b = b \circ a$ for all a, b in S. (The combination table must be symmetrical about the leading diagonal.)

Isomorphism

If the structure of two sets S and T under operations ∘ and * respectively is the same then $(S, \circ)$ and $(T, *)$ are said to be isomorphic. (Note that S and T, and/or ∘ and *, may be identical.)

If $(S, \circ)$ and $(T, *)$ are isomorphic then there is a correspondence between elements of S and T, written $x \leftrightarrow a$, such that

- all elements of S and T are paired in this way;
- if $x \leftrightarrow a$ and $y \leftrightarrow b$ then $x \circ y \leftrightarrow a * b$.

There may be more than one isomorphism between sets! Under any isomorphism, the identity elements **must** correspond to each other.

■ Write out combination tables for sets:

$A = \{1, 3, 5, 7\}$ under 'x mod 10'
B = symmetries set of the rectangle shown
$C = \{0, 1, 2, 3\}$ under '+ mod 4'.

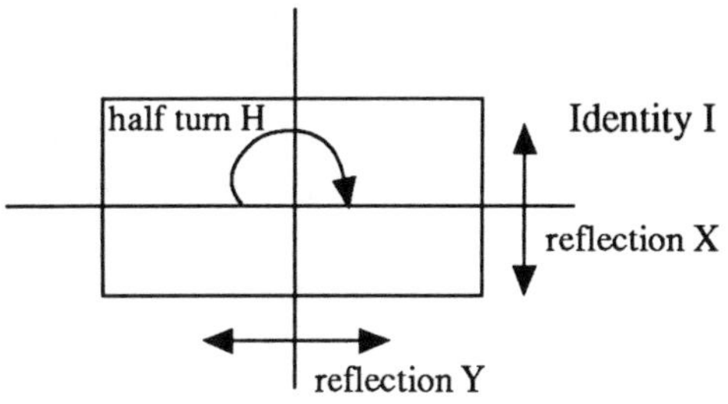

Check for identity elements and which operations are commutative. Are any (or all) of these sets isomorphic?

● *A*

x	1	3	7	9
1	1	3	7	9
3	3	9	1	7
7	7	1	9	3
9	9	7	3	1

B

∘	I	H	X	Y
I	I	H	X	Y
H	H	I	Y	X
X	X	Y	I	H
Y	Y	X	H	I

C

+	0	1	2	3
0	0	1	2	3
1	1	2	3	0
2	2	3	0	1
3	3	0	1	2

Identities are 1, I and 0. All tables are symmetric in leading diagonal (commutative). *B* has the identity along the leading diagonal – the other two do not. To see that *A* and *C* are isomorphic, *A* can be rewritten as follows.

x	1	3	9	7
1	1	3	9	7
3	3	9	7	1
9	9	7	1	3
7	7	1	3	9

then $1 \leftrightarrow 0$
$3 \leftrightarrow 1$ (or 3)
$9 \leftrightarrow 2$
$7 \leftrightarrow 3$ (or 1)

For example,
$3 \times 9 = 7$
↕ ↕ ↕
$1 + 2 = 3$

Note: All these operations **are** associative.

1 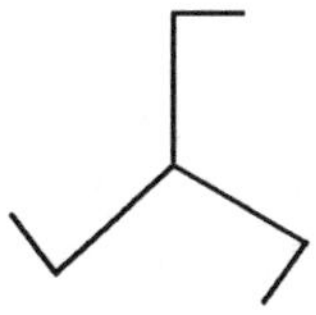

Denoting rotations of 120°, 240° and 360° by *a*, *b*, *c* respectively, draw up a combination table for the symmetries set of the triquetra. What is the identity element?

2 Draw up a combination table for {0, 1, 2} under 'addition mod 3'. Is this isomorphic to the set described in question 1?

3 Let the operation *G* be 'choose the larger of'. For example, 3 *G* 4 = 4, 5 *G* 2 = 5, 1 *G* 1 = 1. Construct a table for this operation on the set {1, 2, 3, 4, 5}. Is *G* commutative? Is there an identity?

4 The operation ~ is defined on {0, 1, 2, 3, 4 ...} by $x \sim y = |x - y|$ (the modulus or positive value of $x - y$ e.g. $|3 - 4| = 1$, $|5 - 2| = 3$). Is it commutative? Is it associative? Is there an identity?

5 Investigate the sets:

$A = \{0, 1, 2, 3, 4\}$ under operation '+ mod 5'.
B = **rotational** symmetries of a pentagon.

6 A new rule ⊕ is defined on the set of integers, by:

$$a \oplus b = a + b + 1, \text{ where + is normal addition.}$$

Find the identity under ⊕. Is ⊕ commutative? Is ⊕ associative?

7 Consider the set of all linear functions of the form $f(x) = ax + b$ where a and b are real numbers. The operation 'addition' is defined by:

$$[f + g](x) = f(x) + g(x)$$

Prove that this operation is both commutative and associative. Investigate whether an identity exists.

8 By considering two specific linear functions, show that the combination of functions under the function of a function rule is not commutative. What is the identity for the set of linear functions under this rule?

Set notation

Venn diagrams are frequently used to represent information in a form that will help to solve problems.

ε	: the universal set
$C \subseteq B$	: C is a subset of B
$B \supseteq C$	: B contains the set C
$A \cap B$	: the intersection of sets A and B
$A \cup B$	: the union of sets A and B
A'	: the complement of set A
$n(A)$	: the number of elements in set A
$x \in A$	: x is an element of the set A
$y \notin B$	: y is not an element of the set B
$\varnothing$	: the empty set or the null set

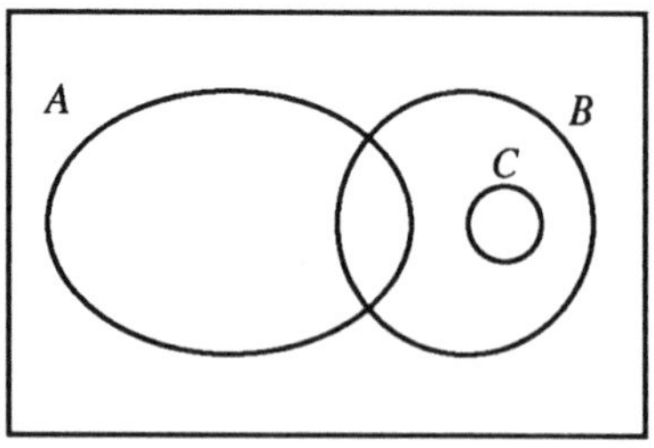

Boolean algebra

Idempotent laws	$A \cup A = A$	: $A \cap A = A$
Identity laws	$A \cup \varnothing = A$	: $A \cap \varepsilon = A$
	$A \cup \varepsilon = \varepsilon$	: $A \cap \varnothing = \varnothing$
Complement laws	$A \cup A' = \varepsilon$	: $A \cap A' = \varnothing$
	$\varepsilon' = \varnothing$	: $\varnothing' = \varepsilon$
	$(A')' = A$	
Commutative laws	$A \cup B = B \cup A$	: $A \cap B = B \cap A$
Associative laws	$A \cup (B \cup C) = (A \cup B) \cup C$	: $A \cap (B \cap C) = (A \cap B) \cap C$
Distributive laws		
	$A \cup (B \cap C) = (A \cup B) \cap (A \cup C)$	: $A \cap (B \cup C) = (A \cap B) \cup (A \cap C)$
De Morgan's laws	$(A \cup B)' = A' \cap B'$	: $(A \cap B)' = A' \cup B'$

The principle of duality says that if you swap $\cap$ with $\cup$ and ε with $\varnothing$ in any identity, then you produce another valid identity.

Switching circuits

The structure of sets and switches are isomorphic and therefore any circuit can be replaced by a Boolean expression. This expression may then be simplified using any of the laws of Boolean algebra in order to produce a new simpler switching circuit which is the equivalent of the original circuit.

Sets of numbers

$\mathbb{N}$ is the set of natural numbers e.g. 1, 2, 3, ...

$\mathbb{Z}$ is the set of integers e.g. ..., –2, –1, 0, 1, 2, ...

$\mathbb{Q}$ is the set of rational numbers or numbers than can be expressed as ratios of integers.

$\mathbb{R}$ is the set of real numbers.

Infinity

Countability: A set is countable if you can pair off elements of the set with elements of the natural numbers.

Cardinality: Elements of the set $\{S, L, U, G\}$ can be paired off with elements of $\{1, 2, 3, 4\}$ and so this set is countable, with cardinality 4.

The cardinality of $\mathbb{N}$ is said to be $\aleph_0$. $\mathbb{Z}$ and $\mathbb{Q}$ also have cardinality $\aleph_0$, but $\mathbb{R}$ is not countable.

On a Venn diagram illustrate the following regions:

■ (a) $(A \cup B)'$

(b) $A \cap (B' \cup C)$

● (a)

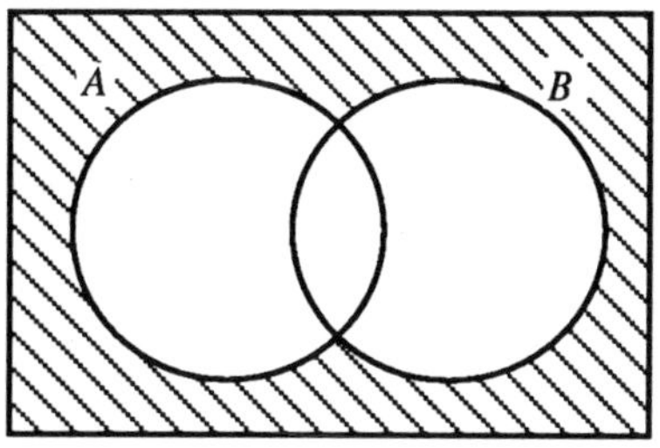

(b)

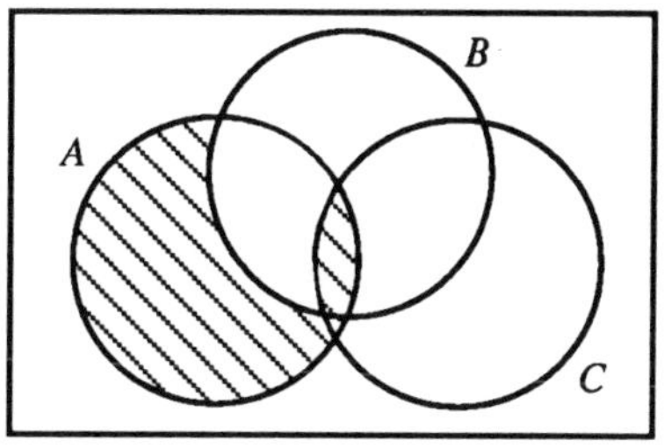

■ Use the axioms of Boolean algebra to simplify:
$(A \cap B) \cup (A' \cap B)$

● $= (B \cap A) \cup (B \cap A')$ *Commutative law*

$= B \cap (A \cup A')$ *Distributive law*

$= B \cap \varepsilon$ *Complement law*

$= B$ *Identity law*

■ Write down the dual of the following Boolean expressions:

(a) $A \cap (A' \cup B)$

(b) $(B \cap \varepsilon) \cap (B' \cap \varnothing)$

● (a) $A \cup (A' \cap B)$

(b) $(B \cup \varnothing) \cup (B' \cup \varepsilon)$

■ Draw the circuit which is represented by the Boolean expression:

$$(a \cap b) \cup (a \cap b')$$

Apply the distributive law to

$$(a \cap b) \cup (a \cap b')$$

Hence or otherwise, simplify this expression and draw an equivalent simplified version of the original circuit.

●

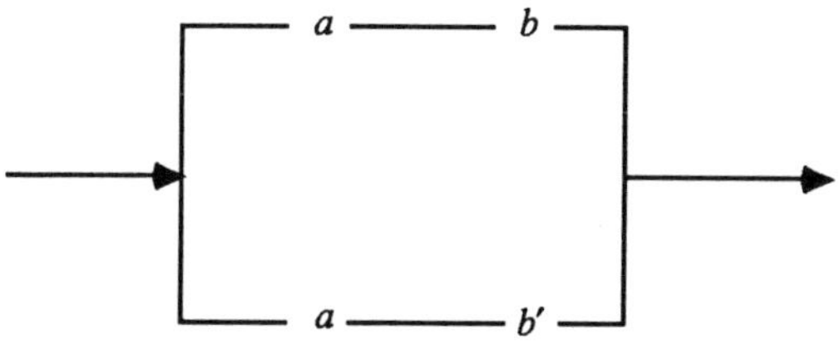

$(a \cap b) \cup (a \cap b')$

$= a \cap (b \cup b')$ *Distributive law*

$= a \cap \varepsilon$ *Complement law*

$= a$ *Identity law*

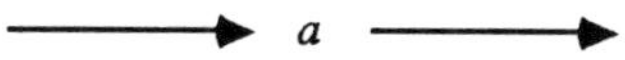

1 On a Venn diagram illustrate the following regions:

(a) $A' \cap B$

(b) $A' \cup (B \cap C)$

2 Use the axioms of Boolean algebra to simplify:

$$(A' \cup B) \cap (A \cup B)$$

3 Write down the dual of the following Boolean expressions:

(a) $(A \cup B)' \cap \varnothing$

(b) $(A \cup \varepsilon) \cup (A' \cap \varnothing)$

4 Use the axioms of Boolean algebra to simplify:

$$(a \cup b')' \cap b$$

5 (a) Draw the switching circuit which is represented by the Boolean expression:

$$[p \cap (p' \cup q)] \cup [q \cap (p \cup q')]$$

(b) Simplify this expression and hence draw an equivalent simplified version of the original circuit.

6 Two relay switches control a switching circuit.

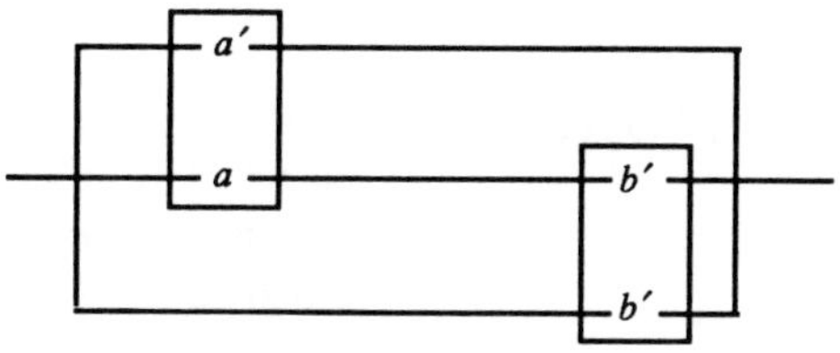

(a) Write down the Boolean expression which represents this circuit.

(b) Use the basic axioms to simplify this expression.

Groups

A group G is any set of elements with a binary operation such that:

$ab \in G$ for all $a, b \in G$	closure
$(ab)c = a(bc)$ for all $a, b, c \in G$	associativity
There is an element e of G such that $ae = ea = a$ for all $a \in G$	identity
For each element $a \in G$ there is an element a^{-1} such that $aa^{-1} = a^{-1}a = e$	inverse

Combination tables

For any set of elements and binary operation a combination table may be formed by combining the elements of the set.

	a	b	c
a	a^2	ab	ac
b	ba	b^2	bc
c	ca	cb	c^2

The combination table for a group is known as a group table and has the latin square property: each element of the group occurs once and only once in each row and column of the table.

Cancellation laws

If a, b and c are elements of a group then:

(i) $ab = ac$ implies $b = c$
(ii) $ba = ca$ implies $b = c$

Symmetry groups

A symmetry of an object is a transformation which leaves the object unchanged. In two dimensions, the symmetries of a shape will consist of:

- the identity transformation **I**;
- reflections in all the lines of symmetry;
- rotations which map the shape onto itself.

Subgroups

A group contained within another group is called a subgroup.

Any element a of a finite group with identity e generates a cyclic subgroup $\{a, a^2, a^3 \dots\}$. The number of elements in this subgroup is the smallest power of a which equals the identity. This number is called the order of a.

Lagrange's theorem

If a group G has n elements it is said that the group is of order n. This is denoted as $|G|$. Lagrange's theorem states that if H is a subgroup of G then $|H|$ divides $|G|$.

Fermat's Little Theorem follows from this. This says that for any integer a and prime number p, $a^p - a$ is divisible by p.

Classifying

Two groups are isomorphic if they are the same apart from the labelling of their elements. Any group with a prime number of elements is cyclic. It follows therefore that any group of order p where p is prime will be isomorphic to $\mathbb{Z}_p$. So there is only one group of each order 2, 3, 5, 7, etc.

- The only group of order 1 is $\{e\}$.
- There are two groups of order 4: the cyclic group and the Klein group.
- There are two groups of order 6: the cyclic group and the group S_3 of permutations of three numbers.

■ Which of the following constitutes a group? Justify your answer.

(a) The set $\{a, b, c\}$ with a binary operation and the following combination table:

	a	b	c
a	b	a	b
b	a	b	c
c	b	c	a

(b) The set of real numbers with the binary operation of multiplication.

(c) The set of non-zero real numbers with the binary operation of multiplication.

● (a) is clearly not a group since it fails to obey the latin square principle. Associativity is not satisfied, since $a(ac) = ab = a$ but $(aa)c = bc = c$.

(b) Zero has no inverse. Therefore this cannot be a group.

(c) is closed since the product of two non-zero reals is a non-zero real. 1 is the identity and any real $x \neq 0$ has an inverse $\frac{1}{x}$. You know that multiplication is associative. Hence this does form an infinite group.

■ What are the symmetries of the following shape? Draw a combination table for these symmetries and say to which known group the symmetry group is isomorphic. Also state the order of each element of the group.

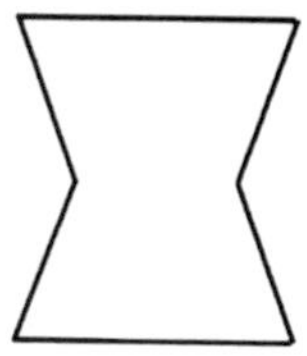

● There are two lines of symmetry; one vertical and one horizontal. Denote reflection in these lines by **L** and **M** respectively.

There is one possible rotation of 180° about the centre of the shape. Denote this **R**. The combination table is

	I	**L**	**M**	**R**
I	**I**	**L**	**M**	**R**
L	**L**	**I**	**R**	**M**
M	**M**	**R**	**I**	**L**
R	**R**	**M**	**L**	**I**

Since the group is of order 4 and clearly not cyclic it must be K, the Klein group.

I is of order 1. **L** is of order 2 since $\mathbf{L}^2 = \mathbf{I}$. Similarly, **M** and **R** are of order 2.

1 Form the combination table of the set $\{3, 6, 9, 12\}$ under multiplication modulo 15. Use it to show that this is in fact a group, stating the identity element and inverses. Find all subgroups of this group and identify the known group to which it is isomorphic. Also find the order of each element of the group.

2 Does the set $\{1, a, b, c, d\}$ with the combination table below form a group? Justify your answer.

	1	a	b	c	d
1	1	a	b	c	d
a	a	c	d	b	1
b	b	1	c	d	a
c	c	d	a	1	b
d	d	b	1	a	c

3 Give the group tables for the symmetries of each of the shapes below. State, giving your reason, whether the two groups are isomorphic.

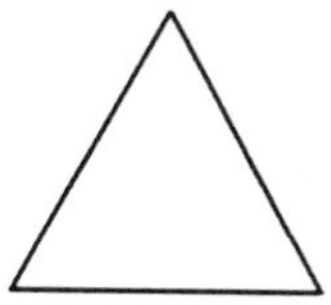

4 (a) Prove that $a^7 - a$ is divisible by $14a$ where a is any odd integer not divisible by 7. You may assume Fermat's Little Theorem.

(b) Deduce a similar result for $a^{11} - a$. Generalise your result for any prime.

5 A group contains an element r of order 4 and a self-inverse element s such that $rs = sr^3$. Decide how many elements are in the subgroup generated by r and s and draw up the group table.

6 (a) Show that a group of order 25 must contain a cyclic subgroup of order 5.

(b) Show that a group of order 16 must contain a cyclic subgroup of order 2.

(c) Show that a group of order p^n where p is prime and n is an integer must contain a cyclic subgroup of order p.

7 List all the possibilities for subgroups of a group of order 8.

8 Prove that, if a and b are members of a group, the inverse of ab must be $b^{-1}a^{-1}$.

9 Does the set of non-zero real numbers under the binary operation of division form a group? Justify your answer.

What is a 'proof'?

A proof presents a convincing and rigorous argument based on factual evidence and logical reasoning which supports a given proposition. There are a number of ways in which a proof may be made in mathematics and some of the more important of these are discussed below.

Direct methods

These might include, for example, direct algebraic proof or a proof made by considering every possibility (a 'proof by exhaustion'). In such proofs great care must be taken to ensure that all cases are considered and that nothing is overlooked.

Notice that a single **counterexample** is sufficient to **disprove** a statement. For example, consider the proposition:

> Numbers that end in 4 are divisible by 4.
> 14 is not divisible by 4 and so the statement is false.

Note that the fact that there are an infinite number of cases where the proposition is true (4, 24, 44, 64, ... are all divisible by 4) does not prove the result.

Demonstrating that a proposition is correct in a large (or even infinite) number of cases is never sufficient to prove the result.

Proof by contradiction

Here the approach is to consider the alternative(s) to what you wish to prove and then to proceed to show that this leads to a **contradiction**. A good example is the proof that $\sqrt{2}$ is irrational.

Suppose that $\sqrt{2} = \frac{a}{b}$ where a and b are whole numbers. You can suppose further that a and b have no common factors. In particular, they cannot both be even.

Then $\quad 2 = \frac{a^2}{b^2}$

$\Rightarrow 2b^2 = a^2$

Therefore a^2 is even and so ***a* must be even.**

Let $\quad a = 2c$

$\Rightarrow 2b^2 = 4c^2$

$\Rightarrow b^2 = 2c^2$

Therefore b^2 is even and so ***b* must be even.**

This contradiction of the fact that a and b are not both even means that $\sqrt{2}$ must be irrational.

Proof by axiom

A proof can be constructed by using a set of axioms that are true by definition or have already been proved. Euclidean geometry is a classic example, as are many of the proofs you encountered in the chapter on groups.

Inductive proof

In an inductive proof you show that:

- P(1) is true
- P(k + 1) is true when P(k) is true

The proposition is then true for all integer values of k.

■ Show that $9^n - 1$ is divisible by 8 for all positive integers n.

● This proof may be made by mathematical induction.

You are trying to prove that the result holds when $n = 1, 2, 3, 4, \ldots$ and for all integer values of n.

$9^1 - 1 = 8$ is divisible by 8 and so P(1) is true.

Assume that P(k) is true.

Then $9^k - 1 = 8M$ (where M is an integer)

$$\begin{aligned} 9^{k+1} - 1 &= 9 \times 9^k - 1 \\ &= 9(8M + 1) - 1 \\ &= 72M + 9 - 1 \\ &= 72M + 8 \\ &= 8 \times (9M + 1) \end{aligned}$$

This is divisible by 8 and so P(k + 1) is true whenever P(k) is true.

Since P(1) is true then the result is true for all positive integers.

This completes the proof by mathematical induction.

■ Prove that $1^2 + 2^2 + 3^2 + \ldots + n^2 = \dfrac{n(n+1)(2n+1)}{6}$

● The result may be proved by induction.

When $n = 1$ the result is true since $1^2 = 1 = \dfrac{1 \times 2 \times 3}{6}$

Now assume that P(k) is true i.e.

$$1^2 + 2^2 + 3^2 + \ldots + k^2 = \frac{k(k+1)(2k+1)}{6}$$

Then the sum of the first $k + 1$ squares is

$$\underbrace{1^2 + 2^2 + 3^2 + \ldots + k^2}_{\downarrow} + (k+1)^2$$

$$= \boxed{\frac{k(k+1)(2k+1)}{6}} + (k+1)^2$$

$$= \frac{(k+1)}{6}[k(2k+1) + 6(k+1)] \qquad \text{factorising}$$

$$= \frac{(k+1)}{6}[2k^2 + 7k + 6] \qquad \text{simplifying}$$

$$= \frac{(k+1)(k+2)(2k+3)}{6} \qquad \text{factorising}$$

Hence P(k + 1) is true.

You have shown that P(k + 1) is true if P(k) is true. Since P(1) is true then the result is true for all positive integer values of n.

1 Show that

$$1.1! + 2.2! + 3.3! + \ldots + n.n! = (n+1)! - 1$$

2 Prove that

$$\frac{d}{dx}(x^n) = nx^{n-1}$$

3 Show that $n^3 - n$ is a multiple of 3 for all positive integer values of n.

4 Show that

$$\sum_1^n r(r+1) = \frac{1}{3}n(n+1)(n+2)$$

5 Show that the sum of $1^2 + 3^2 + 5^2 + \ldots$ to n terms is $\dfrac{1}{3}n(4n^2 - 1)$.

6 Show that numbers of the form $4^n - 3n - 1$ are always divisible by 9 for all integer $n (n \geq 1)$.

7 Prove that

$$1.6 + 2.7 + 3.8 + \ldots + n(n+5) = \frac{n}{3}(n+1)(n+8)$$

8 Show that

$$\frac{0}{1!} + \frac{1}{2!} + \frac{2}{3!} + \frac{3}{4!} + \ldots + \frac{n-1}{n!} = 1 - \frac{1}{n!}$$

9 Find a counterexample for each of the following conjectures.

(a) $n^2 + n + 41$ is prime for all positive integers n.

(b) For positive integers a and b, the square of the mean of a and b is greater than the product of a and b.

(c) At a minimum point on a graph the gradient is zero.

(d) The product of two irrational numbers is always irrational.

(e) It is impossible to place 8 queens on a chessboard so that no 2 of them are in the same straight line (horizontal, vertical or diagonal).

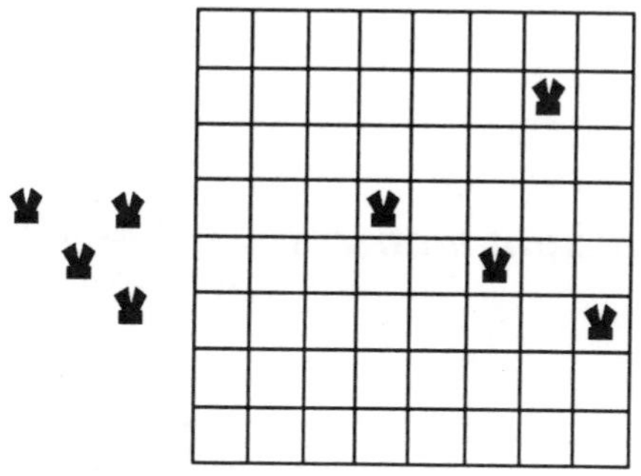

MATRICES

Data storage

Data presented in a two-way table is called an **array** or **matrix**.

A 2 x 3 matrix has 2 rows and 3 columns and can be shown:

$$\begin{bmatrix} a_{11} & a_{12} & a_{13} \\ a_{21} & a_{22} & a_{23} \end{bmatrix}$$

In general each entry is an **element** and a_{mn} is the element in the mth row and nth column.

A 2 x 3 matrix is said to have **order** 2 x 3.

Matrix arithmetic

(a) To add (or subtract) matrices, just add (or subtract) the corresponding elements. So if **A** is a matrix with elements a_{ij} , **B** with elements b_{ij} then:

$$\mathbf{C} = \mathbf{A} + \mathbf{B} \text{ if } c_{ij} = a_{ij} + b_{ij} \quad \text{for all } i \text{ and } j$$

It follows that addition or subtraction of matrices is **only** possible if the matrices to be combined have the **same order**.

(b) To multiply (or divide) a matrix by a scalar, multiply (or divide) each element in the matrix by the scalar. For example:

$$3\begin{bmatrix} 2 & 5 \\ 0 & 1 \end{bmatrix} = \begin{bmatrix} 6 & 15 \\ 0 & 3 \end{bmatrix}$$

Matrix multiplication

If the number of columns in the first matrix is equal to the number of rows in the second matrix, then the matrices can be combined in an operation known as matrix multiplication.

$$\begin{bmatrix} \cdot & \cdot & \cdot \\ a_{21} & a_{22} & a_{23} \\ \cdot & \cdot & \cdot \end{bmatrix} \begin{bmatrix} b_{11} & \cdot \\ b_{21} & \cdot \\ b_{31} & \cdot \end{bmatrix} = \begin{bmatrix} \cdot & \cdot \\ c_{21} & \cdot \\ \cdot & \cdot \end{bmatrix}$$

where $c_{21} = a_{21}b_{11} + a_{22}b_{21} + a_{23}b_{31}$.

Note that if a 3×3 matrix is multiplied by a 3×2 matrix then the result is a 3×2 matrix.

$$(3 \times 3)\,(3 \times 2) = (3 \times 2)$$

the same

Note also that matrix multiplication is associative but **not** commutative.

Transition matrices

These are used to represent situations in which the outcome depends in some way upon the preceding state.

A process in which each subsequent event depends upon its preceding event is called a **stochastic process**. For example, if vector **a** is initial state, **T** is a matrix, **Ta** is next state, $\mathbf{T}^2\mathbf{a}$ is the following state, etc.

■ $\begin{bmatrix} 2 & 3 & 1 \\ 0 & 1 & 2 \end{bmatrix}\begin{bmatrix} 1 \\ 5 \\ 0 \end{bmatrix}$

● $\begin{bmatrix} 17 \\ 5 \end{bmatrix} \begin{matrix} \leftarrow 2\times 1 + 3\times 5 + 1\times 0 \\ \leftarrow 0\times 1 + 1\times 5 + 2\times 0 \end{matrix}$

■

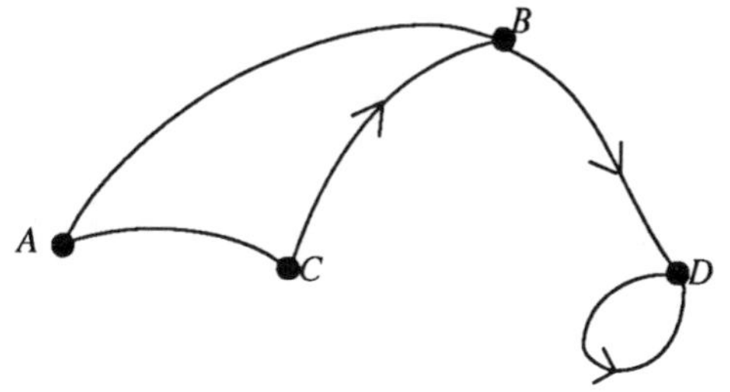

(a) Draw a matrix, **T**, to represent this network.

(b) What does $\mathbf{T}^2$ represent?

● (a)

		From			
		A	*B*	*C*	*D*
To	*A*	0	1	1	0
	B	1	0	1	0
	C	1	0	0	0
	D	0	1	0	1

(b) The number of **two-stage** routes between each pair of points on the network.

■ Suppose that rain one day means there is a $\frac{4}{5}$ chance of rain the next day but that if it is dry there is only a $\frac{2}{5}$ chance of rain the next day.

(a) Write down a transition matrix for the situation.

(b) If it rains today, what is the probability it rains on the third day from now?

● (a)

$$\begin{matrix} & R & D \\ R & \frac{4}{5} & \frac{2}{5} \\ D & \frac{1}{5} & \frac{3}{5} \end{matrix}$$

So $\mathbf{T} = \frac{1}{5}\begin{bmatrix} 4 & 2 \\ 1 & 3 \end{bmatrix}$

(b) So $\mathbf{T}^3 = \frac{1}{125}\begin{bmatrix} 18 & 14 \\ 7 & 11 \end{bmatrix}\begin{bmatrix} 4 & 2 \\ 1 & 3 \end{bmatrix}$

$= \frac{1}{125}\begin{bmatrix} 86 & 78 \\ 39 & 47 \end{bmatrix}$

So $\mathbf{T}^3\begin{bmatrix} 1 \\ 0 \end{bmatrix} = \frac{1}{125}\begin{bmatrix} 86 \\ 39 \end{bmatrix}$

P(rain on third day) $= \frac{86}{125}$

1 Give an example to show that multiplication of 2×2 matrices is not commutative.

2

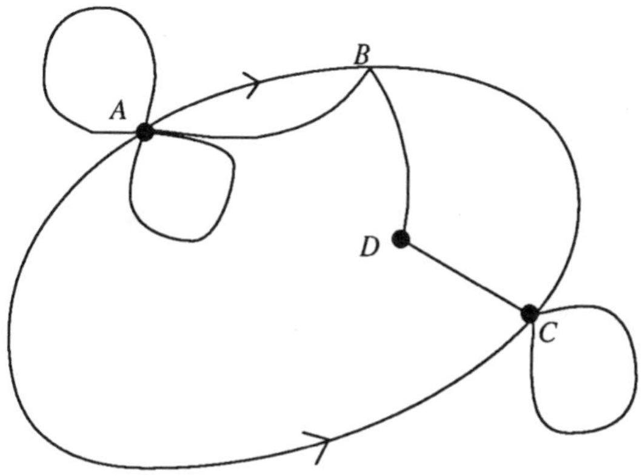

(a) Draw a matrix, **M**, to represent single-stage routes on this network.

(b) (i) What does $\mathbf{M}^2$ represent?

(ii) Evaluate $\mathbf{M}^2$.

3 $\mathbf{A} = \begin{bmatrix} 1 & 2 \\ 3 & 1 \end{bmatrix}$ $\mathbf{B} = \begin{bmatrix} -1 & 0 \\ 0 & -1 \end{bmatrix}$ $\mathbf{C} = \begin{bmatrix} 0 & 5 \\ 6 & 0 \end{bmatrix}$

Calculate: (a) **A** + 2**B** (b) **AC**

(c) **AB** (d) **CA**

4 $\mathbf{T} = \begin{bmatrix} 0.7 & 0.5 \\ 0.3 & 0.5 \end{bmatrix}$ is a transition matrix representing the conditional probability of rain tomorrow where $\begin{bmatrix} 1 \\ 0 \end{bmatrix}$ is rain today and $\begin{bmatrix} 0 \\ 1 \end{bmatrix}$ is no rain.

(a) If it rains today, what is the probability of rain tomorrow?

(b) If it does not rain today, what is the probability of rain tomorrow?

(c) If it rains today, what is the probability of rain in 3 days' time?

(d) Estimate, to 1 decimal place, the possibility of rain in *n* days' time, where *n* is a large number. Why does this not depend on whether it rains today or not?

Transformations

Reflections, rotations, translations, stretches, enlargements, shears, etc. can be described **geometrically.** For example, for a rotation give the **centre** and **angle of rotation.**

Linear transformations

These satisfy the following conditions:

- $\mathbf{T}(\lambda\mathbf{a}) = \lambda\mathbf{T}(\mathbf{a})$
- $\mathbf{T}(\mathbf{a} + \mathbf{b}) = \mathbf{T}(\mathbf{a}) + \mathbf{T}(\mathbf{b})$

for any vectors **a** and **b** and any real number λ.

They can be represented by 2×2 matrices such that if $\begin{bmatrix} 1 \\ 2 \end{bmatrix}$ is an object point then under the transformation $\begin{bmatrix} 2 & 0 \\ 0 & 4 \end{bmatrix}$, a two-way stretch, $\begin{bmatrix} 1 \\ 2 \end{bmatrix}$ maps to $\begin{bmatrix} 2 & 0 \\ 0 & 4 \end{bmatrix}\begin{bmatrix} 1 \\ 2 \end{bmatrix} = \begin{bmatrix} 2 \\ 8 \end{bmatrix}$.

Key transformation matrices

(a) Two-way stretch, centre (0, 0), factor a in the x-direction, factor b in the y-direction $\begin{bmatrix} a & 0 \\ 0 & b \end{bmatrix}$

It follows that an enlargement, centre (0, 0), factor a, can be represented by: $\begin{bmatrix} a & 0 \\ 0 & a \end{bmatrix}$

(b) Shear, x-axis invariant, $(0, 1) \to (k, 1)$ $\begin{bmatrix} 1 & k \\ 0 & 1 \end{bmatrix}$

(c) Rotation of θ anti-clockwise about (0, 0) $\begin{bmatrix} \cos\theta & -\sin\theta \\ \sin\theta & \cos\theta \end{bmatrix}$

(d) Reflection in $y = x\tan\theta$ $\begin{bmatrix} \cos 2\theta & \sin 2\theta \\ \sin 2\theta & -\cos 2\theta \end{bmatrix}$

Special case: Reflection in $y = x$. Substitute $\theta = \frac{\pi}{4}$ in the above, giving: $\begin{bmatrix} 0 & 1 \\ 1 & 0 \end{bmatrix}$

Combinations of transformations

If P represents an object, **T** a transformation, then $P' = \mathbf{T}(P)$ represents the **image** of P under transformation **T**.

If **S** is another transformation, then $P'' = \mathbf{S}(\mathbf{T}(P))$ is the image obtained by starting with P, applying **T** to it and then **S** to the result.

For brevity, you write $\mathbf{ST}(P)$ to mean the result of **T then S** on P.

Inverses

If $\mathbf{T}(P) = P'$, then the **inverse** of transformation **T** (written $\mathbf{T}^{-1}$) is such that $\mathbf{T}^{-1}(P') = P$. Then $\mathbf{T}^{-1}\mathbf{T}(P) = P$ i.e. $\mathbf{T}^{-1}$ reverses the effect of **T**.

If the **matrix** for **T** is $\begin{bmatrix} a & b \\ c & d \end{bmatrix}$, then, providing $|\mathbf{T}| \neq 0$,

$$\mathbf{T}^{-1} = \frac{1}{|\mathbf{T}|}\begin{bmatrix} d & -b \\ -c & a \end{bmatrix},$$

where $|\mathbf{T}| = ad - bc$ is the **determinant** of **T**.

■ A linear transformation maps $\begin{bmatrix}1\\0\end{bmatrix} \to \begin{bmatrix}2\\0\end{bmatrix}$ and $\begin{bmatrix}0\\1\end{bmatrix} \to \begin{bmatrix}0\\3\end{bmatrix}$

(a) Describe this transformation geometrically.

(b) Write down the 2×2 matrix **M** which represents this transformation.

(c) Find $\mathbf{M}^{-1}$.

(d) Describe the transformation represented by $\mathbf{M}^{-1}$.

● (a) A two-way stretch, centre (0, 0), factor 2 in the x-direction, factor 3 in the y-direction.

(b) $\mathbf{M} = \begin{bmatrix}2 & 0\\0 & 3\end{bmatrix}$

(c) $\mathbf{M}^{-1} = \frac{1}{6}\begin{bmatrix}3 & 0\\0 & 2\end{bmatrix} = \begin{bmatrix}\frac{1}{2} & 0\\0 & \frac{1}{3}\end{bmatrix}$

(d) $\mathbf{M}^{-1}$ represents the inverse to (a), that is a two-way stretch, centre (0, 0), factor $\frac{1}{2}$ in the x-direction, factor $\frac{1}{3}$ in the y-direction.

■ (a) Write down the matrix, **S**, for a rotation of 45° anti-clockwise about the origin. Simplify your answer.

(b) Find $\mathbf{S}^{-1}$.

(c) If $\mathbf{T} = \begin{bmatrix}1 & 0\\0 & -1\end{bmatrix}$, describe fully the transformation represented by **T**.

(d) Calculate $\mathbf{S}^{-1}\mathbf{TS}$.

(e) Describe fully the transformation represented by the matrix $\mathbf{S}^{-1}\mathbf{TS}$.

● (a) $\mathbf{S} = \begin{bmatrix}\cos 45° & -\sin 45°\\ \sin 45° & \cos 45°\end{bmatrix} = \frac{\sqrt{2}}{2}\begin{bmatrix}1 & -1\\1 & 1\end{bmatrix}$

(b) $\mathbf{S}^{-1} = \frac{\sqrt{2}}{2}\begin{bmatrix}1 & 1\\-1 & 1\end{bmatrix}$ Rotation of 45° clockwise about (0, 0).

(c) **T** is a reflection in the x-axis.

(d) $\mathbf{S}^{-1}\mathbf{TS} = \begin{bmatrix}0 & -1\\-1 & 0\end{bmatrix}$

(e) Reflection in the line $y = -x$.

1 Write down matrices for the following transformations.

(a) A shear with x-axis invariant such that (0, 1) maps to (2, 1).

(b) A rotation of 30° **clockwise** about the origin.

(c) A reflection in the x-axis.

(d) A reflection in the line $y = 2x$.

2 Write down matrices for inverse transformations for each of the above and describe the inverse transformations geometrically.

3

$\mathbf{S} = \begin{bmatrix}1 & 0\\0 & -1\end{bmatrix}$ $\quad \mathbf{T} = \begin{bmatrix}0 & -1\\1 & 0\end{bmatrix}$

(a) Describe fully the transformations represented by the matrices **S** and **T**.

(b) Find the effect of the transformation **ST** on the point (1, –1). Explain your result.

(c) What is the effect of the transformation **TS** on the point (1, –1)?

(d) Describe the inverses to both transformations **S** and **T** and write down the matrices $\mathbf{S}^{-1}$ and $\mathbf{T}^{-1}$.

4 (a) Describe the transformation represented by the matrix $\mathbf{M} = \begin{bmatrix}2 & 3\\0 & 0\end{bmatrix}$.

(b) What is the value of $|\mathbf{M}|$? (The determinant of **M**). Explain the significance of your result.

5

$$\mathbf{M}_\theta = \begin{bmatrix}\cos 2\theta & \sin 2\theta\\ \sin 2\theta & -\cos 2\theta\end{bmatrix}$$

Calculate $\mathbf{M}_\theta^{\,2}$ and interpret your result geometrically.

6 Consider the matrix

$$\begin{bmatrix}1 & \sqrt{3}\\ -\sqrt{3} & 1\end{bmatrix}$$

By considering its effect on base vectors $\begin{bmatrix}1\\0\end{bmatrix}$ and $\begin{bmatrix}0\\1\end{bmatrix}$ or otherwise, describe fully geometrically the transformation which it represents.

7 Consider the matrix $\mathbf{M} = \begin{bmatrix}1 & 0 & 0\\0 & 1 & 0\\0 & 0 & 0\end{bmatrix}$

Describe fully the transformation represented by **M**.

Simultaneous equations

Simultaneous equations can be solved either geometrically, by drawing graphs and finding the point of intersection, or algebraically. However, they can also be written in matrix form. For example, the equations

$$3x + 4y = 10$$
$$5x - 3y = 7$$

can be written as $\begin{bmatrix} 3 & 4 \\ 5 & -3 \end{bmatrix}\begin{bmatrix} x \\ y \end{bmatrix} = \begin{bmatrix} 10 \\ 7 \end{bmatrix}$

The equations in matrix form can be solved using the inverse of the matrix $\begin{bmatrix} 3 & 4 \\ 5 & -3 \end{bmatrix}$.

So $\begin{bmatrix} x \\ y \end{bmatrix} = \frac{1}{-29}\begin{bmatrix} -3 & -4 \\ -5 & 3 \end{bmatrix}\begin{bmatrix} 10 \\ 7 \end{bmatrix} = \frac{1}{-29}\begin{bmatrix} -58 \\ -29 \end{bmatrix} = \begin{bmatrix} 2 \\ 1 \end{bmatrix}$

So $x = 2$, $y = 1$

In geometrical terms, the lines $3x + 4y = 10$ and $5x - 3y = 7$ intersect at the point (2, 1).

Geometrical ideas

In interpreting 2 simultaneous linear equations with 2 variables as representing 2 lines, there are three possibilities for the number of solutions:

(i) the 2 lines cross at a point giving 1 solution;
(ii) the 2 lines are parallel giving no solutions;
(iii) the 2 equations represent the same line giving infinitely many solutions.

Crushing transformations

Solving the simultaneous equations given by $\begin{bmatrix} 3 & 4 \\ 5 & -3 \end{bmatrix}\begin{bmatrix} x \\ y \end{bmatrix} = \begin{bmatrix} 10 \\ 7 \end{bmatrix}$ can be thought of as finding the points (x, y) which map onto (10, 7) under the transformation represented by the matrix $\begin{bmatrix} 3 & 4 \\ 5 & -3 \end{bmatrix}$.

Thus we need only apply the inverse transformation to (10, 7). However, if the transformation represents a **crushing transformation** then no inverse exists. In these cases there will be either no solutions or infinitely many solutions.

For example $\begin{bmatrix} 4 & 1 \\ 4 & 1 \end{bmatrix}$ maps all points on to the line $y = x$.

$\begin{bmatrix} 4 & 1 \\ 4 & 1 \end{bmatrix}\begin{bmatrix} x \\ y \end{bmatrix} = \begin{bmatrix} 3 \\ 3 \end{bmatrix}$ has infinitely many solutions.

$\begin{bmatrix} 4 & 1 \\ 4 & 1 \end{bmatrix}\begin{bmatrix} x \\ y \end{bmatrix} = \begin{bmatrix} 4 \\ 7 \end{bmatrix}$ has no solutions.

Equations with no solutions are said to be **inconsistent**. Otherwise, they are said to be **consistent**.

Elimination

The method of elimination can be extended to simultaneous equations with more than two variables. However, they can only have a unique solution if there are at least as many equations as variables. You also need to be extremely careful and well organised in presenting your solutions. In general, it is best to proceed as if there is a unique solution and then, if things go wrong, to explain why.

Planes

Just as linear equations with 2 variables represent lines so linear equations with 3 variables can be thought of as planes. There are five possibilities for 3 planes:

(i) all 3 planes are parallel, no solutions;
(ii) 2 planes are parallel, no solutions;
(iii) they form a triangular prism, no solutions;
(iv) they intersect in a line (forming a sheaf), infinitely many solutions;
(v) they intersect at a point, unique solution.

■ Explain geometrically why the equations

$$2x + 3y = 1$$
$$6y = 3 - 4x$$

have no solutions.

● The equations can be rewritten as

$$2x + 3y = 1$$
$$4x + 6y = 3$$

or in matrix form as $\begin{bmatrix} 2 & 3 \\ 4 & 6 \end{bmatrix}\begin{bmatrix} x \\ y \end{bmatrix} = \begin{bmatrix} 1 \\ 3 \end{bmatrix}$.

Now $\begin{bmatrix} 2 & 3 \\ 4 & 6 \end{bmatrix}$ has no inverse so it represents a crushing transformation which maps the plane onto the line $y = 2x$. However, (1, 3) is not on this line so there are no solutions.

■ Show that the planes

$$x + 2y - z = 3$$
$$2x - 3y + z = 4$$
$$5x + 3y - 2z = 13$$

from a sheaf and find the equation of the line of intersection.

● None of the planes are parallel so try elimination.

$$x + 2y - z = 3 \quad \text{(A)}$$
$$2x - 3y + z = 4 \quad \text{(B)}$$
$$5x + 3y - 2z = 13 \quad \text{(C)}$$

(A) + (B) $\qquad 3x - y = 7 \quad$ (D)
$2 \times$ (B) + (C) $\qquad 9x - 3y = 21 \quad$ (E)

(D) and (E) clearly represent the same equation so the planes form a sheaf.

Now $y = 3x - 7$
Substituting for y in (A) you obtain
$z = 7x - 17$

So $\begin{bmatrix} x \\ y \\ z \end{bmatrix} = \begin{bmatrix} x \\ 3x - 7 \\ 7x - 17 \end{bmatrix}$

The equation of the line of intersection is

$$\begin{bmatrix} x \\ y \\ z \end{bmatrix} = \begin{bmatrix} 0 \\ -7 \\ -17 \end{bmatrix} + \lambda \begin{bmatrix} 1 \\ 3 \\ 7 \end{bmatrix}$$

1 The point P is transformed by the matrix $\begin{bmatrix} 2 & -1 \\ 3 & 4 \end{bmatrix}$ to the point P′ (4, 1). Find the coordinates of P.

2 The lines

$$3x + y = a$$
$$4x - y = b$$

intersect at (1, 3). Find the values of a and b.

3 Find the coordinates of A, the point of intersection of the lines:

$$x + y = 7$$
$$y = 2x - 2$$

4 Explain geometrically why the equations

$$x + 3y = 6$$
$$6y = 12 - 2x$$

have infinitely many solutions.

5 For the equations:

$$2x + ay = 3$$
$$bx - y = 4$$

(a) show that $x = \dfrac{3 + 4a}{ab + 2}$ and $y = \dfrac{3b - 8}{ab + 2}$;

(b) explain why if $a = 1$ and $b = -2$ there will be no solutions;

(c) find the solution if $a = 3$ and $b = 4$.

6 Solve:

$$x + y + z = 4$$
$$3x - y + 4z = 10$$
$$2x + 3y - z = 3$$

7 The equations

$$2x + y + 4z = 2$$
$$x - y + 2z = 1$$
$$x + y + az = 1$$
$$3x - 2y + z = -1$$

have a unique solution. Find the solution, and hence the value of a.

8 Find the point of intersection of the planes:

$$x + 2y - z = 8$$
$$3x - y + 2z = 5$$
$$4x + 2y + 3z = -1$$

9 Find the equation of the line of intersection of the three planes:

$$x - y + 2z = 3$$
$$x - 2y + 3z = -4$$
$$2x - 3y + 5z = -1$$

10 Show that the following planes form a prism:

$$3x - y + 2z = 4$$
$$x + y + 5z = 7$$
$$9x + y + 19z = 13$$

Invariant points

An **invariant point** of a transformation is a point which is its own image. The origin is an invariant point for every linear transformation but some transformations have other invariant points as well. For example,

Reflection:	any point on the mirror line;
Shear:	any point on the invariant line.

Invariant points are found by solving:

$$\begin{bmatrix} a & b \\ c & d \end{bmatrix}\begin{bmatrix} x \\ y \end{bmatrix} = \begin{bmatrix} x \\ y \end{bmatrix}$$

Invariant lines, eigenvectors and eigenvalues

An **invariant line** of a transformation is one for which each point on the line maps to a point also on the line (the points on the line need not be invariant points).

An **eigenvector** of **M** is a non-zero vector in the direction of an invariant line. If **e** is an eigenvector then

$$\mathbf{Me} = \lambda\mathbf{e}$$

for some number λ.

The number λ is called the **eigenvalue** of **e** and is the stretch factor parallel to the eigenvector. The eigenvalues are the roots of the **characteristic equation**

$$|\mathbf{M} - \lambda\mathbf{I}| = 0$$

An eigenvector corrresponding to an eigenvalue λ is found by solving:

$$\begin{bmatrix} a & b \\ c & d \end{bmatrix}\begin{bmatrix} x \\ y \end{bmatrix} = \lambda\begin{bmatrix} x \\ y \end{bmatrix} \text{ i.e. } \begin{bmatrix} a-\lambda & b \\ c & d-\lambda \end{bmatrix}\begin{bmatrix} x \\ y \end{bmatrix} = \mathbf{0}$$

Any non-zero solution will do, so it is usual to choose as simple a solution as possible.

Diagonal matrices

A 2×2 **diagonal** matrix is one of the form $\begin{bmatrix} \lambda & 0 \\ 0 & \mu \end{bmatrix}$

It is easy to find powers of a diagonal matrix:

$$\begin{bmatrix} \lambda & 0 \\ 0 & \mu \end{bmatrix}^n = \begin{bmatrix} \lambda^n & 0 \\ 0 & \mu^n \end{bmatrix}$$

Any 2×2 matrix with distinct eigenvalues λ_1 and λ_2 and corresponding eigenvectors $\mathbf{e}_1$ and $\mathbf{e}_2$ can be written as

$$\mathbf{M} = \mathbf{UDU}^{-1}$$

where $\mathbf{U} = \begin{bmatrix} \mathbf{e}_1 & \mathbf{e}_2 \end{bmatrix}$ and $\mathbf{D} = \begin{bmatrix} \lambda_1 & 0 \\ 0 & \lambda_2 \end{bmatrix}$

This can be used to find powers of **M**: $\mathbf{M}^n = \mathbf{UD}^n\mathbf{U}^{-1}$

Cayley-Hamilton theorem

This states that a matrix satisfies its characteristic equation. In other words, if a 2×2 matrix has characteristic equation:

$$ax^2 + bx + c = 0,$$

then **M** satisfies the equation:

$$a\mathbf{M}^2 + b\mathbf{M} + c\mathbf{I} = 0$$

This can be used to find the inverse of **M**, since if you multiply through by $\mathbf{M}^{-1}$ you obtain

$$a\mathbf{M} + b\mathbf{I} + c\mathbf{M}^{-1} = 0$$

It can also be used to find powers of **M** by multiplying through by $\mathbf{M}, \mathbf{M}^2, \ldots$

■ (a) Find the eigenvalues of:

$$\mathbf{M} = \begin{bmatrix} 4 & 3 \\ 2 & -1 \end{bmatrix}$$

(b) For each eigenvalue find an eigenvector.

(c) Describe the transformation geometrically.

(d) Express **M** in the form $\mathbf{UDU}^{-1}$ where **D** is a diagonal matrix.

● (a) $\mathbf{M} - \lambda\mathbf{I} = \begin{bmatrix} 4-\lambda & 3 \\ 2 & -1-\lambda \end{bmatrix}$ so the characteristic equation is:

$$(4-\lambda)(-1-\lambda) - (2)(3) = 0$$
$$\Rightarrow \quad \lambda^2 - 3\lambda - 10 = 0$$

Solving gives eigenvalues $\lambda = 5$ or $\lambda = -2$.

(b) $\begin{bmatrix} 4-5 & 3 \\ 2 & -1-5 \end{bmatrix}\begin{bmatrix} x \\ y \end{bmatrix} = \begin{bmatrix} 0 \\ 0 \end{bmatrix}$

Therefore $\begin{bmatrix} 3 \\ 1 \end{bmatrix}$ is an eigenvector.

Similarly, $\lambda = -2$ gives eigenvector $\begin{bmatrix} 1 \\ -2 \end{bmatrix}$.

(c) Two-way stretch, factor 5 in direction $\begin{bmatrix} 3 \\ 1 \end{bmatrix}$ and -2 in direction $\begin{bmatrix} 1 \\ -2 \end{bmatrix}$

(d) $\mathbf{D} = \begin{bmatrix} 5 & 0 \\ 0 & -2 \end{bmatrix}$ and $\mathbf{U} = \begin{bmatrix} 3 & 1 \\ 1 & -2 \end{bmatrix}$

■ (a) Find the characteristic equation of:

$$\mathbf{M} = \begin{bmatrix} 1 & -k \\ \frac{1}{k} & 0 \end{bmatrix}$$

and deduce that **M** has no invariant lines.

(b) Using the Cayley-Hamilton theorem, find constants a and b such that $\mathbf{M}^2 = a\mathbf{M} + b\mathbf{I}$ and deduce that $\mathbf{M}^3 = -\mathbf{I}$.

● (a) $\mathbf{M} - \lambda\mathbf{I} = \begin{bmatrix} 1-\lambda & -k \\ \frac{1}{k} & -\lambda \end{bmatrix}$ so the characteristic equation is

$$(1-\lambda)(-\lambda) - \left(\frac{1}{k}\right)(-k) = 0$$

which simplifies to $\lambda^2 - \lambda + 1 = 0$.

This equation has no real roots (how can you tell?) therefore no eigenvalues or eigenvectors and no invariant lines.

(b) By the Cayley-Hamilton theorem:

$$\mathbf{M}^2 - \mathbf{M} + \mathbf{I} = 0$$
$$\Rightarrow \quad \mathbf{M}^2 = \mathbf{M} - \mathbf{I}$$

Therefore
$$\begin{aligned}\mathbf{M}^3 &= \mathbf{M}(\mathbf{M} - \mathbf{I}) \\ &= \mathbf{M}^2 - \mathbf{M} \\ &= (\mathbf{M} - \mathbf{I}) - \mathbf{M} \\ &= -\mathbf{I}\end{aligned}$$

1 For each of the following transformations state (i) the invariant points and (ii) the invariant lines.

(a) Reflection in the y-axis.

(b) Rotation of 180° about the origin.

(c) Two-way stretch $\begin{bmatrix} 2 & 0 \\ 0 & 1 \end{bmatrix}$.

2 A linear transformation has matrix $\mathbf{A} = \begin{bmatrix} 1 & 1 \\ 4 & -2 \end{bmatrix}$.

(a) Find the eigenvalues of **A**.

(b) For each eigenvalue, find an eigenvector.

(c) Describe the transformation geometrically.

(d) Find a matrix **U** and a diagonal matrix **D** such that $\mathbf{A} = \mathbf{UDU}^{-1}$.

3 Find the characteristic equation of $\mathbf{T} = \begin{bmatrix} 2\sqrt{2} & 5 \\ -1 & -\sqrt{2} \end{bmatrix}$ and deduce that **T** has no invariant lines.

Using the Cayley-Hamilton theorem, find numbers a and b such that $\mathbf{T}^2 = a\mathbf{T} + b\mathbf{I}$ and deduce that $\mathbf{T}^4 + \mathbf{I} = 0$.

4 A matrix **M** has eigenvectors $\begin{bmatrix} 2 \\ 1 \end{bmatrix}$ and $\begin{bmatrix} 1 \\ 1 \end{bmatrix}$ with eigenvalues 3 and -1 respectively.

Write down a diagonal matrix **D** and a matrix **U** such that $\mathbf{M} = \mathbf{UDU}^{-1}$. Hence find constant matrices **A** and **B** such that for any integer n:

$$\mathbf{M}^n = 3^n\mathbf{A} + (-1)^n\mathbf{B}$$

5 The transformation **T** has matrix $\begin{bmatrix} 3 & p \\ 4 & q \end{bmatrix}$.

(a) Given that $y = x$ is an invariant line of **T**, write down an eigenvector and show that $p - q = 1$.

(b) Given that $y + 2x = 0$ is another invariant line, find another equation in p and q. Hence find their values.

6 Show that, whatever the value of k, the matrix $\begin{bmatrix} 1 & k \\ 4k & 1 \end{bmatrix}$ has an eigenvector $\begin{bmatrix} 1 \\ 2 \end{bmatrix}$, and find, in terms of k, the corresponding eigenvalue. Find also the other eigenvector and eigenvalue.

Gaussian elimination

A set of n linear equations in n unknowns can be represented conveniently in a table or extended matrix form. Row operations, of multiplying any row by a non-zero constant or adding a multiple (positive or negative) of one row to another row, are used to produce a set of simpler equations which have the same solution. Gaussian elimination is a systematic method of eliminating variables.

Algorithm:

(a) choose the coefficient of the first variable in the first equation as the pivot; (Partial pivoting is usually used as this reduces possible errors due to rounding. This involves rearranging the equations so that the equation with the largest absolute value of coefficient is first.)

(b) using the pivot, eliminate the first variable from the remaining equations by subtracting multiples of the first equation;

(c) repeat steps (a) and (b) to eliminate the second variable;

(d) continue until just one variable remains;

(e) use back substitution to find each variable in turn.

LU decomposition

This can be used in solving a set of equations expressed in the form: $\mathbf{Ax} = \mathbf{b}$

Express $\mathbf{A}$ as $\mathbf{LU}$ where $\mathbf{L}$ and $\mathbf{U}$ are lower and upper triangular matrices respectively.

$$\mathbf{Ax} = \mathbf{b} \Rightarrow \mathbf{LUx} = \mathbf{b} \Rightarrow \mathbf{L(Ux)} = \mathbf{b}$$

Let $\mathbf{y} = \mathbf{Ux}$ then solve $\mathbf{Ly} = \mathbf{b}$ (by using forward substitution, because $\mathbf{L}$ is lower triangular) and then solve $\mathbf{Ux} = \mathbf{y}$ (by using back substitution because $\mathbf{U}$ is upper triangular).

Gauss Seidel method

This is an iterative method of solving a set of linear equations. The method does not always converge and the ordering of the equations is usually important for convergence. The method is particularly good if there are many zero coefficients in off-diagonal terms. It can be shown that the method will converge if, for each row, the magnitude of the coefficent of the term on the diagonal is greater than the sum of the magnitudes of the other coefficients. Always try to rearrange the equations so that there is a strong leading diagonal.

The following equations have a strong leading diagonal:

$$10x + y = 28$$
$$x + 10y + z = 49.9$$
$$y + 5z = -7$$

The iterative formulas: $x_{n+1} = \dfrac{28 - y_n}{10}$, $y_{n+1} = \dfrac{49.9 - x_{n+1} - z_n}{10}$, $z_{n+1} = \dfrac{(-7 - y_{n+1})}{5}$

with starting values, say, $x_1 = 0$, $y_1 = 0$, $z_1 = 0$ will therefore converge rapidly to the solution $x = 2.300$, $y = 5.000$, $z = -2.400$.

Ill-conditioned equations

A set of linear equations is ill-conditioned if small changes in one or more of the coefficients of the variables or constants leads to large changes in the solution set. Ill-conditioning can lead to problems when solving equations by machine, where there may be rounding or truncation errors in the storage of the coefficients.

When solving two equations in two unknowns, ill-conditioning will occur when the gradients of the lines which give a geometrical interpretation of the equations have almost equal gradients, as small changes in one of the gradients, possibly brought about by a small change in one of the coefficients, can lead to large changes in the solution.

■ Solve the following equations using Gaussian elimination.

$$\begin{aligned} 5x_1 + 4x_2 + 2x_3 &= 6 \\ 2x_1 - 2x_2 + 3x_3 &= -10 \\ x_1 + 8x_2 + 3x_3 &= -2 \end{aligned}$$

● Using tabular form:

x_1	x_2	x_3	c	Equation number
5	4	2	6	①
2	−2	3	−10	②
1	8	3	−2	③
0	−3.6	2.2	−12.4	④ = ② − 0.4 ①
0	7.2	2.6	−3.2	⑤ = ③ − 0.2 ①

Rearrange the order of the equations (i.e. use partial pivoting).

x_1	x_2	x_3	c	Equation number
0	7.2	2.6	−3.2	⑤
0	−3.6	2.2	−12.4	④
0	0	3.5	−14	⑥ = ④ + 0.5 ⑤

From ⑥,

$$3.5x_3 = -14$$
$$\Rightarrow \quad x_3 = -4$$

Using back substitution:

From ⑤, $x_2 = 1$

From ①, $x_1 = 2$

The solution is:

$$x_1 = 2, \quad x_2 = 1, \quad x_3 = -4$$

1 Use Gaussian elimination, with partial pivoting, to solve the following equations.

$$\begin{aligned} 2x_1 + 2x_2 + 4x_3 + 5x_4 &= 12 \\ 2x_1 + 3x_2 + 5x_3 + x_4 &= -7 \\ x_1 - x_2 + 6x_3 + 2x_4 &= -2 \\ x_1 + 2x_2 + 5x_3 + 2x_4 &= -3 \end{aligned}$$

2 Use Gaussian elimination, with partial pivoting, to solve the equations:

$$\begin{aligned} 6.60x_1 + 7.20x_2 + 3.55x_3 &= 38.75 \\ 3.96x_1 + 11.17x_2 + 3.68x_3 &= 44.70 \\ 1.32x_1 + 4.18x_2 + 1.57x_3 &= 17.53 \end{aligned}$$

3 Use the LU decomposition method to solve the equations:

$$\begin{aligned} 2x_1 + x_2 + x_3 &= 1 \\ x_1 + 4x_2 + 2x_3 &= -11 \\ 2x_1 - x_2 + 5x_3 &= 10 \end{aligned}$$

4 Use the LU decomposition method to solve the equations:

$$\begin{aligned} 5x_1 + 2x_2 + x_3 &= 5 \\ x_1 + 3x_2 + 2x_3 &= -2.5 \\ 3x_1 - 4x_2 + 5x_3 &= -14.8 \end{aligned}$$

5 Solve the equations from the above worked example using the LU decomposition method:

$$\begin{aligned} 5x_1 + 4x_2 + 2x_3 &= 6 \\ 2x_1 - 2x_2 + 3x_3 &= -10 \\ x_1 + 8x_2 + 3x_3 &= -2 \end{aligned}$$

6 Use the Gauss Seidel method to solve the equations:

$$8x - 3y = 9, \quad 20y + 3z = 79, \quad x - 10z = 73$$

7 Solve the equations:

$$\begin{aligned} 5z - 2w &= 9.6 \\ x + 8w &= 43.8 \\ 10x + y &= 22.6 \\ 8y + z &= 8.8 \end{aligned}$$

(The Gauss Seidel method is particularly appropriate here because of the strong leading diagonal when the equations are reordered and the number of zero coefficients of variables in the equations.)

8 Investigate whether the following equations are ill-conditioned by making small changes in the coefficients of x.

$$\begin{aligned} 5.5x + 3.0y &= 96.0 \\ 13.6x + 7.4y &= 237.2 \end{aligned}$$

9 In the following two sets of equations the coefficients of x and y are given to 3 decimal places. Investigate the conditioning of the equations by considering the solution sets when the coefficients are rounded to 1 decimal place.

(a) $3.225x + 4.183y = 115.9$
$6.386x - 8.246y = -101.1$

(b) $3.225x + 4.183y = 115.9$
$6.386x + 8.246y = -101.1$

Canonical form

Any matrix equation of the form:

$$\mathbf{T(x) = y}$$

may be written in an extended matrix form:

$$\left[\mathbf{T} \;\vdots\; \mathbf{y}\right]$$

and then, in most cases, reduced by row operations to a canonical form of the type:

$$\left[\begin{array}{c:c:c} \mathbf{I} & \mathbf{K} & \mathbf{P} \\ \hdashline \mathbf{0} & \mathbf{0} & \mathbf{0} \end{array}\right]$$

where **I** is the identity matrix.

■ $$\begin{bmatrix} 2 & -4 & 1 \\ 1 & 3 & -1 \\ 1 & -17 & 5 \end{bmatrix} \begin{bmatrix} x \\ y \\ z \end{bmatrix} = \begin{bmatrix} 4 \\ -6 \\ 26 \end{bmatrix}$$

Reduce this equation to canonical form.

● $$\left[\begin{array}{ccc:c} 2 & -4 & 1 & 4 \\ 1 & 3 & -1 & -6 \\ 1 & -17 & 5 & 26 \end{array}\right]$$

(K) ↓ (P) ↓

$$\left[\begin{array}{cc:c:c} 1 & 0 & -1/10 & -6/5 \\ 0 & 1 & -3/10 & -8/5 \\ \hdashline 0 & 0 & 0 & 0 \end{array}\right]$$

Kernels

The kernel, K, is the solution set of the equation:

$$\mathbf{T(x) = 0}$$

When K is non-zero it is the set of all vectors which are crushed onto the origin by the transformation. It may be a line, a plane or a larger set depending on how many dimensions are crushed.

■ Find the kernel of the equation given above.

● $$\begin{bmatrix} 1 & 0 & -1/10 \\ 0 & 1 & -3/10 \end{bmatrix} \mathbf{k} = \mathbf{0}$$

$$\Rightarrow \mathbf{k} = \lambda \begin{bmatrix} 1 \\ 3 \\ 10 \end{bmatrix}, \text{ for } \lambda \in \mathbb{R}$$

Particular solution

This is a solution to the equation:

$$\mathbf{T(p) = y}$$

■ Find a particular solution to the equation given above.

● $$\mathbf{p} = \begin{bmatrix} -6/5 \\ -8/5 \\ 0 \end{bmatrix}$$

General solution

All solutions are of the form:

$$\mathbf{x = p + k}$$

where **p** is a particular solution and **k** is the kernel.

If K is only one-dimensional then $K = \{\lambda \mathbf{k}\}$ and the general solution is

$$\mathbf{x} = \mathbf{p} + \lambda \mathbf{k}$$

which is the general equation of a straight line.

■ Find the solution for all the points which are crushed by **T** to the point

$$\mathbf{y} = \begin{bmatrix} 4 \\ -6 \\ 26 \end{bmatrix}$$

● $$\mathbf{x} = \begin{bmatrix} -6/5 \\ -8/5 \\ 0 \end{bmatrix} + \lambda \begin{bmatrix} 1 \\ 3 \\ 10 \end{bmatrix}$$

Categories of solution

Infinitely many solutions: the general method above illustrates how to find these.

Unique solution: when the kernel contains only **0** then there is only the particular solution, in other words a unique answer.

No solution: when a bottom row or rows of zeros are established then the particular solution must also be zero in that row, or it is inconsistent and no solution can exist.

For example:

$$\left[\begin{array}{ccc:c} 1 & 0 & 0 & 1 \\ 0 & 1 & 0 & 4 \\ 0 & 0 & 1 & 3 \end{array}\right]$$

Only the zero vector is in the kernel. The equations have a unique solution.

$$\left[\begin{array}{ccc:c} 1 & 0 & -3 & 4 \\ 0 & 1 & 1 & 1 \\ \hdashline 0 & 0 & 0 & 2^* \end{array}\right]$$

These equations have no solution. The * value must be zero for a solution to exist.

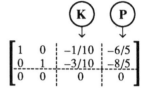

■ For the equation

$$\begin{bmatrix} 2 & 3 & -2 & 1 \\ 1 & -2 & 5 & -1 \\ 5 & -3 & a & -2 \end{bmatrix}\begin{bmatrix} x \\ y \\ z \\ t \end{bmatrix} = \begin{bmatrix} 1 \\ 9 \\ b \end{bmatrix}$$

(a) Explain why there cannot be a unique solution.

(b) Show that when $a = 13$ the transformation crushes two dimensions.

(c) (i) Find the value of b which gives a solution when $a = 13$.

(ii) Hence write down this solution, describing it geometrically.

● (a) This transformation maps a point in 4 dimensions onto one in 3 dimensions so at least one dimension is being crushed. If a solution exists it must be at least a line, so no unique solution can exist.

(b) The extended matrix is

$$\left[\begin{array}{cccc|c} 2 & 3 & -2 & 1 & 1 \\ 1 & -2 & 5 & -1 & 9 \\ 5 & -3 & 13 & -2 & b \end{array}\right]$$

$$\begin{matrix} 2② - ① \\ 2③ - 5① \end{matrix} \Rightarrow \left[\begin{array}{cccc|c} 2 & 3 & -2 & 1 & 1 \\ 0 & -7 & 12 & -3 & 17 \\ 0 & -21 & 36 & -9 & 2b-5 \end{array}\right]$$

$$\begin{matrix} 7① + 3② \\ ③ - 3② \end{matrix} \Rightarrow \left[\begin{array}{cccc|c} 14 & 0 & 22 & -2 & 58 \\ 0 & -7 & 12 & -3 & 17 \\ 0 & 0 & 0 & 0 & 2b-56 \end{array}\right]$$

$$\begin{matrix} 1/14\ ① \\ -1/7\ ② \end{matrix} \Rightarrow \left[\begin{array}{cccc|c} 1 & 0 & 11/7 & -1/7 & 29/7 \\ 0 & 1 & -12/7 & 3/7 & -17/7 \\ 0 & 0 & 0 & 0 & 2b-56 \end{array}\right]$$

The kernel consists of two base vectors

$\begin{bmatrix} -11 \\ 12 \\ 7 \\ 0 \end{bmatrix}$ and $\begin{bmatrix} 1 \\ -3 \\ 0 \\ 7 \end{bmatrix}$, which means that two dimensions are crushed.

(c) (i) For a solution to exist,

$$2b - 56 = 0$$
$$b = 28$$

(ii) The solution is

$$\mathbf{r} = \begin{bmatrix} 29/7 \\ -17/7 \\ 0 \\ 0 \end{bmatrix} + \lambda\begin{bmatrix} -11 \\ 12 \\ 7 \\ 0 \end{bmatrix} + \mu\begin{bmatrix} 1 \\ -3 \\ 0 \\ 7 \end{bmatrix}$$

which is the equation of a plane.

1 For the simultaneous equations:

$$3x + y = 2$$
$$x - 3y - 2z = -6$$
$$x + 2y + z = 4$$

(a) Write down an appropriate extended matrix.

(b) Reduce this matrix to canonical form.

(c) Write down the kernel of the solution.

(d) Write down a particular solution.

(e) Write down the general solution.

2 The transformation **T** transforms from 4-dimensional space and is represented by:

$$\mathbf{T} = \begin{bmatrix} 1 & 7 & -9 & 1 \\ 3 & 1 & 1 & -1 \\ 1 & 2 & -2 & 0 \end{bmatrix}$$

(a) Find the kernel of **T**.

(b) How many dimensions are crushed by **T**?

(c) Find the general solution to the equation

$$\mathbf{T}(\mathbf{r}) = \begin{bmatrix} -3 \\ 7 \\ 1 \end{bmatrix}$$

3 By reducing to canonical form, solve the simultaneous equations:

$$3x - y - z = 3$$
$$x + 3y - 7z = 1$$
$$x - y + z = 1$$

4 Reduce the following simultaneous equations to canonical form.

$$x - 2y - z = 4$$
$$5x - 2y - 3z = 6$$
$$3x - 2y - 2z = 3$$

Hence explain why there can be no solution to these equations.

5 The transformation **M** is represented by the matrix

$$\mathbf{M} = \begin{bmatrix} 1 & -3 & 1 \\ 2 & -1 & a \\ 1 & -8 & -1 \end{bmatrix}$$

(a) For what values of a does a solution exist?

(b) If $\mathbf{M}(\mathbf{r}) = \begin{bmatrix} -2 \\ b \\ -15 \end{bmatrix}$

(i) For what values of a and b do no solutions exist?

(ii) For what values of a and b are there infinitely many solutions? Find the general solution in this case.

COMPLEX NUMBERS

Argand diagram

The real number line can be extended to a plane of points called the **Argand diagram.** This plane is denoted by ℂ. The points in this plane represent **complex numbers.**

Modulus-argument form

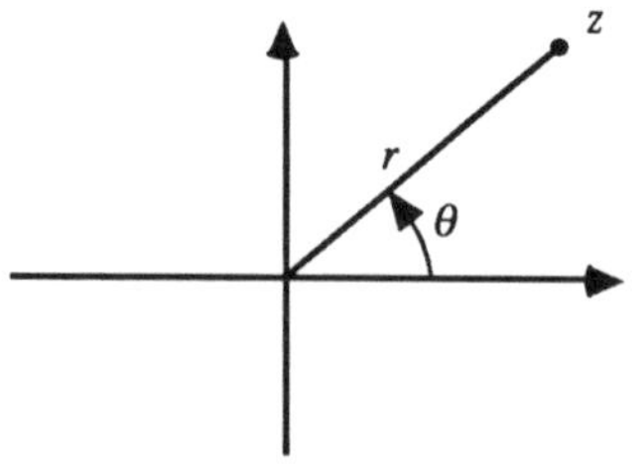

The distance r is called the **modulus,** $|z|$.

The angle θ is called the **argument,** arg (z). (This angle should be given in the range $-180° < \arg(z) \le 180°$ or $-\pi < \arg(z) \le \pi$)

The coordinates $[r, \theta]$ are said to be in **modulus-argument form** (or **polar form**)

If $z_1 = [r_1, \theta_1]$ and $z_2 = [r_2, \theta_2]$ then $z_1z_2 = [r_1r_2, \theta_1 + \theta_2]$ and

$$\frac{z_1}{z_2} = \left[\frac{r_1}{r_2}, \theta_1 - \theta_2\right]$$

The number *j*

Multiplying by the number $j = [1, 90°]$ has the geometrical effect of rotating a complex number 90° about the origin. Two applications of this number are equivalent to a rotation of 180° i.e. $j^2 = -1$.

Cartesian form

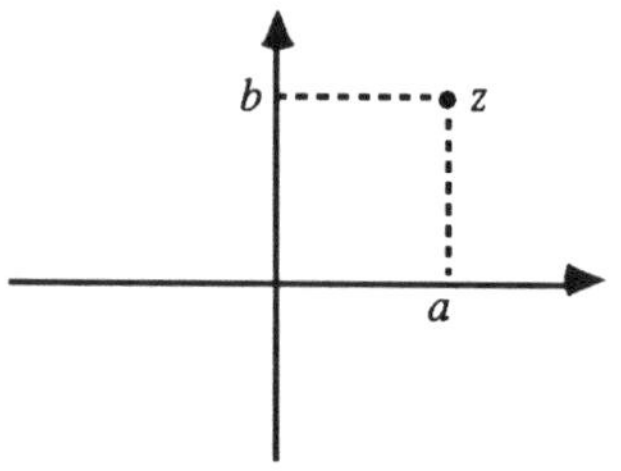

When the complex number z is written in Cartesian form as $a + bj$, then

a is called the **real part** of z

b is called the **imaginary part** of z.

Arithmetical operations can be carried out in Cartesian form:

$$(a + bj) + (c + dj) = (a + c) + (b + d)j$$
$$(a + bj) - (c + dj) = (a - c) + (b - d)j$$
$$(a + bj)(c + dj) = ac + bcj + adj + bdj^2$$
$$= (ac - bd) + (bc + ad)j$$

Polar and Cartesian forms

A sketch and some elementary trigonometry enables one form to be converted to another.

■ Convert [5, –120°] into Cartesian form.

● $a = 5 \cos 60° = 2.5$
$b = 5 \sin 60° \approx 4.33$
$z \approx -2.5 - 4.33j$

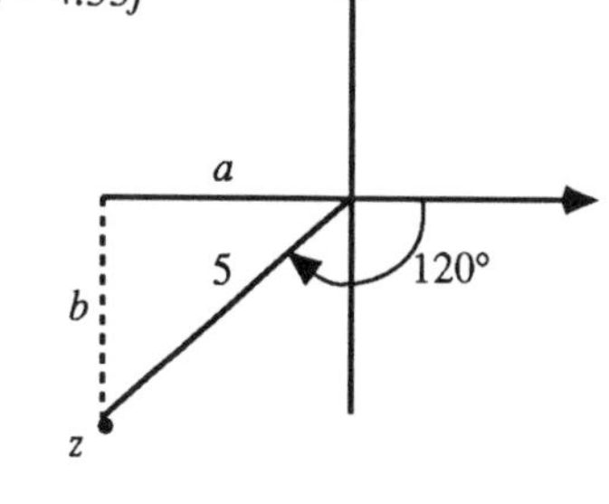

■ Write $-4 + 3j$ in polar form.

● $|z| = \sqrt{(4^2 + 3^2)} = 5$
$\arg z = 180° - \tan^{-1}(3/4)$
$\approx 143.1°$
$z \approx [5, 143.1°]$

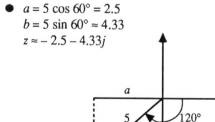

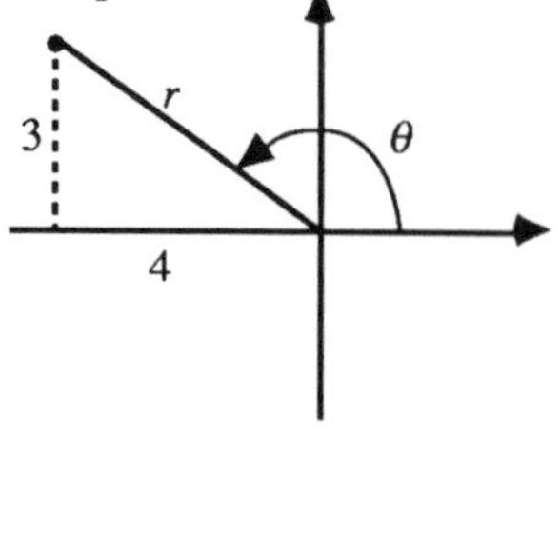

■ Solve $x^2 - 4x + 13 = 0$.

● $x = \dfrac{4 \pm \sqrt{(16 - 4 \times 1 \times 13)}}{2} = \dfrac{4 \pm \sqrt{-36}}{2}$

$x = \dfrac{4 \pm 6j}{2} = 2 \pm 3j$

■ Simplify $(2 - 3j)(7 + 2j)$.

● $14 + 4j - 21j - 6j^2$
$= 14 - 17j + 6 = 20 - 17j$

■ If $z_1 = 1 - j$ and $z_2 = -2j$, find the modulus and argument of:

(a) $z_1 z_2$ (b) $z_2^{\,3}$ (c) $\dfrac{z_1}{z_2}$

● $z_1 = [\sqrt{2}, -45°]$ $z_2 = [2, -90°]$

(a) $z_1 z_2 = [2\sqrt{2}, -135°]$

(b) $z_2^{\,3} = [8, -270°] = [8, 90°]$

(c) $\dfrac{z_1}{z_2} = [\dfrac{\sqrt{2}}{2}, \ 45°]$

■ Simplify: (a) j^4 (b) j^{10}

● (a) $j^4 = (j)^2 = (-1)^2 = 1$

(b) $j^{10} = j^4 \times j^4 \times j^2 = 1 \times 1 \times -1 = -1$

■ Simplify $\left(\dfrac{\sqrt{3}}{2} - \dfrac{1}{2}j\right)^5$ giving the answer in both polar and Cartesian form.

●

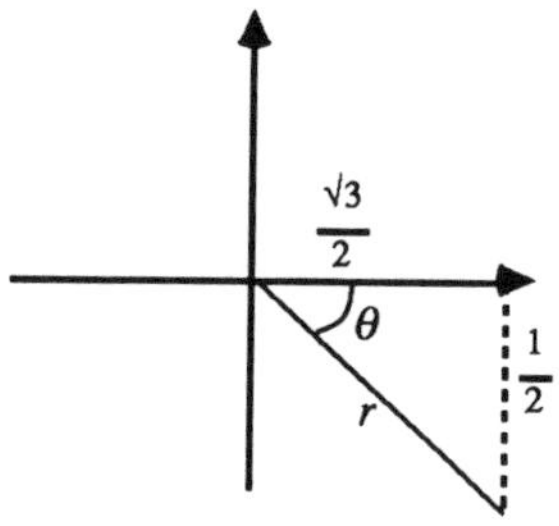

$z = [1, -30°]$

$z^5 = [1, -30°]^5 = [1, -150°]$

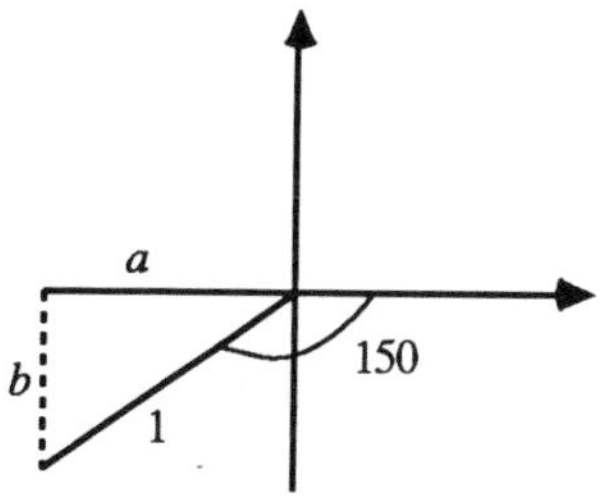

In Cartesian form,

$a = 1 \cos 30° = \dfrac{\sqrt{3}}{2}$

$b = 1 \sin 30° = \dfrac{1}{2}$

$z = -\dfrac{\sqrt{3}}{2} - \dfrac{1}{2}j$

1 If $z = 5 - 3j$ and $w = 2 + 6j$, simplify:

(a) $z + w$ (b) zw (c) z^2

2 Solve the quadratic equation

$$x^2 - 10x + 29 = 0$$

giving the solutions in Cartesian form.

3 Simplify $(1 - \sqrt{3}j)^5$, giving the answer in Cartesian form.

4 The complex numbers z and w satisfy the simultaneous equations

$$2z - 3w = 7 - 11j$$
$$3z + 4w = 19 - 8j$$

Find z and w.

5 Simplify

$$\left(\frac{1}{2} - \frac{\sqrt{3}}{2}j\right)^4 - \left(\frac{1}{2} + \frac{\sqrt{3}}{2}j\right)^4$$

6 The complex number $z = 1 + cj$, where c is a real constant, is such that z^3 is a real number.

Prove that $c^3 - 3c = 0$ and hence find all possible values of z. Find the modulus and argument of z for each possible value of c.

7 Expand $(2 + j)(5 - 3j)(2j - 1)$.

8 Solve the quadratic equation

$$x^2 - 2ax + (a^2 + 4b^2) = 0$$

where a and b are constants.

9 $z = 2 - 2j$ and $w = 1 + j$. Find in polar form:

(a) z^4 (b) $\dfrac{z^4}{w}$ (c) $\dfrac{1}{z}$

10 (a) Prove

$$\sin(90 + \theta) = \cos\theta$$
$$\cos(90 + \theta) = -\sin\theta$$

(b) Hence, if $z = r(\cos\theta + j\sin\theta)$, prove jz represents a rotation of the original complex number through 90° about the origin.

11 (a) Convert $[5, 150°]$ to Cartesian form.

(b) Convert $3j - 1$ to polar form.

12 $z = [2, \theta]$ and $w = [8, \pi - 2\theta]$ where $\tan\theta = \dfrac{3}{4}$. Write in Cartesian form:

(a) zw (b) z^2

Fundamental theorem

The polynomial equation $P_n(z) = 0$ (i.e. the polynomial equation in which z^n is the highest power) has exactly n complex roots e.g. $z^3 + z + 8 = 0$ has 3 roots (zeros).

Quadratic equations

These can be solved using

$$x = \frac{-b \pm \sqrt{(b^2 - 4ac)}}{2a}$$

$b^2 - 4ac$ is called the **discriminant.**

■ Solve $z^2 - 2z + 5 = 0$

● $z = \dfrac{2 \pm \sqrt{(4-20)}}{2}$

$= \dfrac{2 \pm 4j}{2} = 1 \pm 2j$

Complex conjugates

If $z = a + jb$ then the complex conjugate is given by $z^* = a - jb$. It follows from this that $z + z^* = 2a$ and $zz^* = a^2 + b^2$. Geometrically, z^* is the reflection of z in the real axis. The complex conjugate is useful in the division of complex numbers: simply multiply the top and bottom of the given fraction by the conjugate of the bottom.

■ Find $\dfrac{1+3j}{2-j}$

● $\dfrac{1+3j}{2-j} \times \dfrac{2+j}{2+j} = \dfrac{2-3+6j+j}{4+1}$

$= \dfrac{1}{5}(-1+7j)$

Roots of polynomial equations

Any polynomial equation **with real coefficients** has roots which are real or occur in conjugate pairs. For example, $z^3 + z^2 + z + 8 = 0$ must have 3 roots and these will either be all real or one will be real and the other two a conjugate pair. Given the roots of a polynomial equation you can write down the equation. For example, if a quadratic equation has roots $a \pm bj$ it is $z^2 + 2az + (a^2 + b^2) = 0$.

■ Find a polynomial equation with roots 1, 2 and j.

● $(z-1)(z-2)(z-j) = 0$

■ Find the quadratic equation with roots $3 \pm 2j$.

● $z^2 - 2 \times 3z + (3^2 + 2^2) = 0$
i.e. $z^2 - 6z + 13 = 0$

De Moivre's theorem

$(\cos\theta + j\sin\theta)^n = \cos n\theta + j\sin n\theta$

This is useful for solving equations of the type $z^n = c$ (e.g. $z^6 = 1 + j$) and for finding powers of complex numbers.

■ Plot the roots of the equation $z^3 = j$ on an Argand diagram.

● Let $z = [r, \theta]$, then $[r^3, 3\theta] = \left[1, \frac{\pi}{2} + 2n\pi\right]$

One root is $\left[1, \frac{\pi}{6}\right]$. All three roots must be equally spaced on a circle centre the origin and so the diagram is as shown.

$z_1 = \left[1, \frac{\pi}{6}\right]$

$z_2 = \left[1, \frac{5\pi}{6}\right]$

$z_3 = \left[1, \frac{3\pi}{2}\right]$

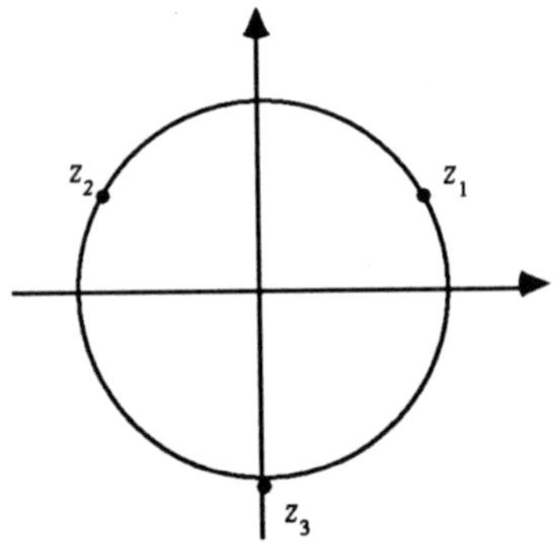

■ Find a cubic equation with roots 2, $1 \pm j$.

● The quadratic with roots $1 \pm j$ is $z^2 - 2z + 2$.

The cubic required is therefore $(z-2)(z^2 - 2z + 2) = 0$
i.e. $z^3 - 4z^2 + 6z - 4 = 0$.

■ Given that $-2 + 3j$ is a root of

$$z^3 + 2z^2 + 5z - 26 = 0$$

find the other roots.

● Since the coefficients are real, another root is $-2 - 3j$. The quadratic with roots $-2 \pm 3j$ is $z^2 + 4z + 13$ and since $(z^2 + 4z + 13)(z - 2) = z^3 + 2z^2 + 5z - 26$, the third root is $z = 2$.

■ Find $(1 + 2j)^5$.

● $(1 + 2j)^5 = [\sqrt{5}, \tan^{-1} 2]^5 = [5^{5/2}, 5\tan^{-1} 2]$

$$= 41 - 38j$$

■ Solve $z^4 = 1 - j$.

● If $z = \left[r, \theta\right]$ and $1 - j = \left[\sqrt{2}, -\frac{\pi}{4}\right]$

$$\left[r, \theta\right]^4 = \left[\sqrt{2}, -\frac{\pi}{4} + 2\pi n\right]$$

$$\Rightarrow \left[r^4, 4\theta\right] = \left[\sqrt{2}, -\frac{\pi}{4} + 2\pi n\right]$$

$$\Rightarrow r = 2^{1/8}, \quad \theta = \frac{\pi n}{2} - \frac{\pi}{16} \quad \text{for } n = 0, 1, 2, 3$$

1 If $z = 4 + 3j$:

(a) write down the value of z^*;

(b) find zz^* and $z + z^*$.

2 Solve:

(a) $z^2 + 4 = 0$

(b) $z^2 - 2z + 2 = 0$

(c) $z^3 + z^2 - 17z + 15 = 0$ given that $z - 3$ is a factor

(d) $z^3 + 8z^2 + 25z + 26 = 0$ given that $-3 + 2j$ is a root

3 Obtain a quadratic equation with roots:

(a) $1 \pm 3j$

(b) $\pm 2j$

(c) $1, j$

4 Find a cubic equation with roots 3, $1 \pm 2j$.

5 Express in the form $a + jb$:

(a) $\dfrac{1+j}{1-j}$

(b) $\dfrac{3-2j}{3+2j}$

(c) $\dfrac{2+3j}{j}$

6 The cubic equation $z^3 + az^2 - 9z + 18j = 0$ has roots $2j$ and ± 3. Find a.

7 If $z = \sqrt{2} + j$, find $\dfrac{1}{z^6}$ in Cartesian form.

8 Solve:

(a) $z^4 = j$

(b) $z^3 = 1 + j$

(c) $(z + 1)^3 = 1 + j$

9 Find the cube roots of -27 in Cartesian form.

10 Find the fourth roots of $1 - j$ in polar form.

11 Solve $z^3 + z^2 j = 0$.

12 Give an equation whose roots z_1 and z_2 are illustrated in the diagram below.

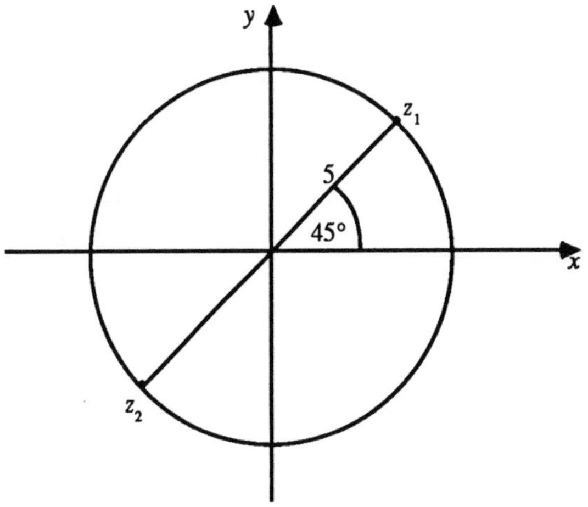

Loci

Sets of points or regions satisfying given conditions can be described by placing restrictions (usually equalities or inequalities) on the complex number z. Such a set of points is called a **locus** (plural loci).

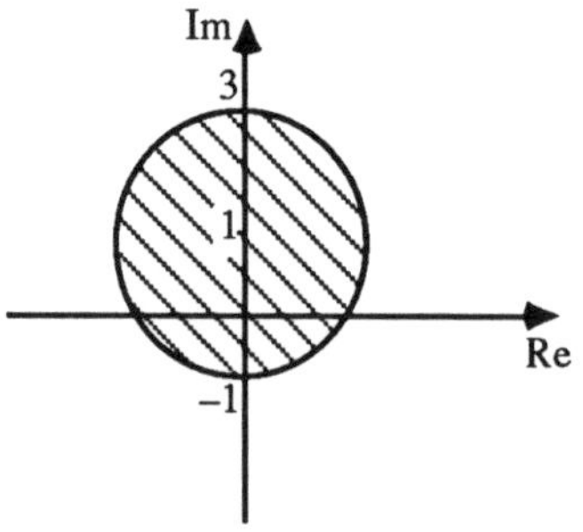

The locus of $\{z : |z - j| \leq 2\}$ is shown. The point representing z in the Argand diagram lies in and on a circle centre (0, 1) and radius 2. Think of $|z - z_1|$ as the distance between the points representing z and z_1.

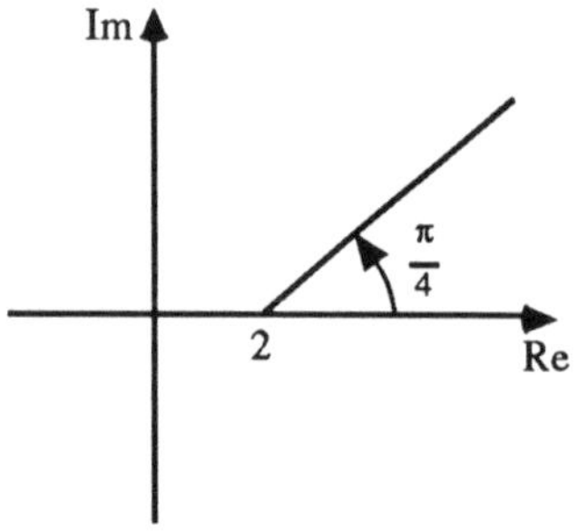

The locus of $\{z : \arg(z - 2) = \frac{\pi}{4}\}$ is the set of points on the half-line shown, excluding (2, 0) where $\arg(z - 2)$ is not defined. Think of $\arg(z - z_1)$ as being the angle the line from z_1 to z makes with the real axis.

Polar graphs

A complex number z can be described in polar form $[r, \theta]$ where $r = |z|$ and $\theta = \arg(z)$. The principal value of θ is the value such that $-180° < \theta \leq 180°$. Polar coordinates can be plotted on a polar grid to give a variety of curves. You might first need to compile a table of values for θ and r.

Complex mappings

Points on an Argand diagram representing z can be mapped onto points in another Argand diagram. By convention, the Argand diagram of the domain is called the z-plane and that for the range is called the ω-plane. u and v are used for the real and imaginary axes in the ω-plane.

$\omega = z + c$	represents a translation through c
$\omega = cz$	represents an enlargement scale factor $\mid c \mid$, centre the origin, and an anti-clockwise rotation through $\arg(c)$
$\omega = z^*$	represents a reflection in the real axis
$\omega = -z^*$	represents a reflection in the imaginary axis

Transformation of loci

A locus of points can be transformed in the z-plane by applying a complex mapping to obtain a new locus in the ω-plane. To find the equation of the new locus:

- investigate the geometrical effect of the transformation using sketches and hence describe the new locus using set notation;

or

- use algebra, substituting for z in terms of ω in the given locus equation.

$z \rightarrow z^n$

Under the mapping $z \rightarrow z^n$ (n is any positive integer), a point $P\ [r, \theta]$ maps onto $P'\ [r^n, n\theta]$.

The solutions of $z^n = c$ consists of n points equally spaced on a circle, centre the origin, radius $|c|^{1/n}$. Once one solution has been found, other solutions are generated by successively increasing the argument by $\frac{2\pi}{n}$.

■ Sketch the locus $\{z : |z - 1 + j| = 1\}$. Find the image of this locus under the transformation $z \to jz^* + 3$. Draw a sketch and give its equation.

●

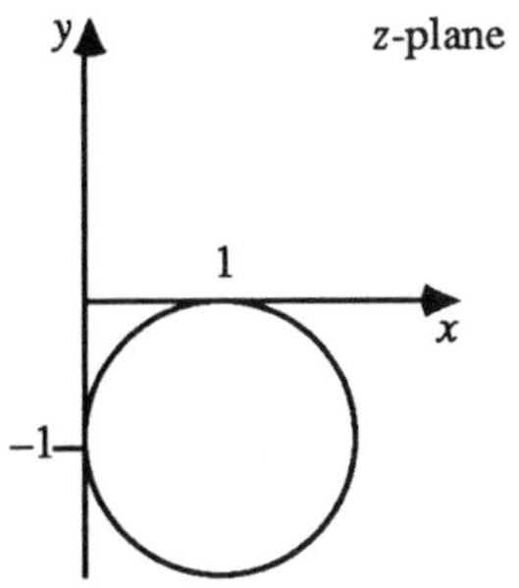

$\{z : |z - 1 + j| = 1\}$
Circle, centre (1, –1), radius 1

$\{\omega : |\omega - 2 - j| = 1\}$
Circle, centre (2, 1), radius 1

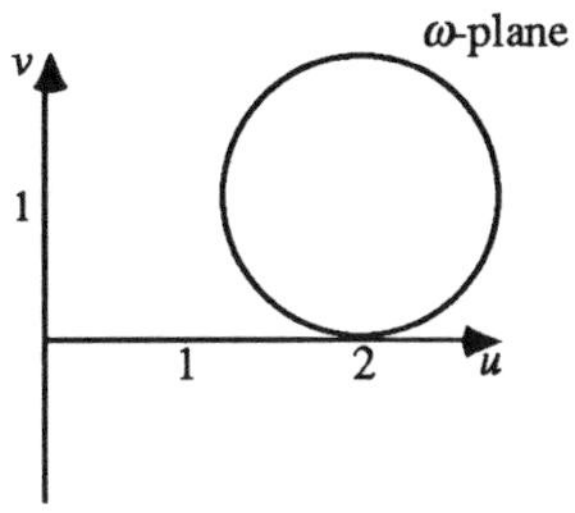

■ Describe the geometrical transformation represented by $z \to jz^* + 3$.

● $z \to z^* \to jz^* \to jz^* + 3$

This is a combination, in order, of:

a reflection in the real axis,

an anti-clockwise rotation of 90° about the origin,

a translation of $\begin{bmatrix} 3 \\ 0 \end{bmatrix}$.

■ Sketch the locus given by $\arg\left(\frac{z}{z-2}\right) = \frac{\pi}{2}$.

● This is a semi-circle with the line from (0, 0) to (2, 0) as diameter, going anti-clockwise from (0, 0) to (2, 0).

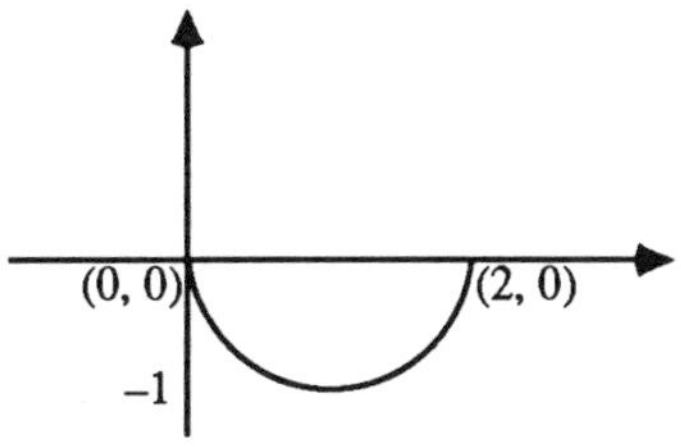

■ State the Cartesian equation of the locus of z if $|z - 2| = |z - 2j|$.

● The locus is the perpendicular bisector of the line joining the points (2, 0) and (0, 2) in the Argand diagram, hence its equation is $y = x$.

■ Describe the locus defined by

$$\arg\left(\frac{z - z_1}{z - z_2}\right) = \theta$$

● This is an arc of a circle with end points z_1 and z_2.

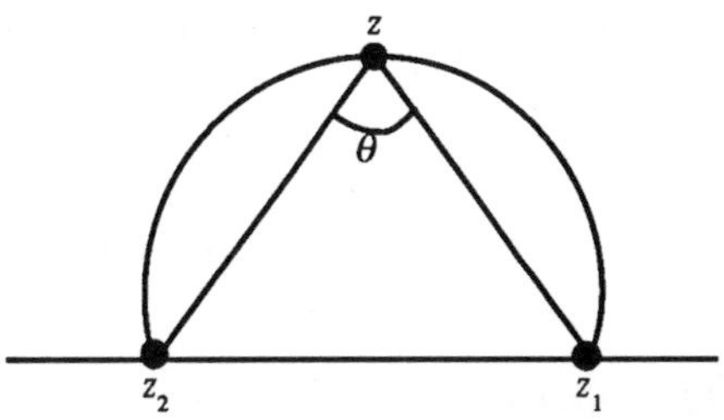

1 Sketch the following loci on Argand diagrams:

(a) $\{z : |z + 2j| \le 1\}$

(b) $\{z : \arg(z - 3) \le 45°\} \cap \{z : \arg(z) \le 30°\}$

(c) $\{z : 0 \le \text{Re}(z) \le 2\} \cap \{z : -1 \le \text{Im}(z) \le 1\}$

2 Use the sketch in question 1(a) to find the range of values of $|z|$. What is the range of values of $\arg(z)$?

3 Sketch the graph of $r = 4 \sin 3\theta$.

4 Find the image of the locus $\{z : \arg(z) = -120°\}$ under the transformation $z \to z^2$.

5 (a) Use substitution to find the equation of the locus $\{z : |z - 1 - 4j| < 2\}$ under the transformation $z \to z(1 - j)$.

(b) Describe, in words, the image set.

6 Give a geometrical description of each of the following. Consider each as a combination of transformations.

(a) $z \to 2z - j$

(b) $z \to j(z - j)$

(c) $z \to (z + 1 - 3j)^*$

(d) $z \to 2j - z^*$

7 Sketch the locus given by $2|z| = |z - 3|$.

(a) By writing $z = x + jy$ express this locus as a Cartesian equation of a circle.

(b) Find its centre and radius.

8 Sketch the locus given by $\arg\left(\frac{z}{z - 3j}\right) = -\frac{\pi}{2}$.

e^z

The exponential function e^z where z is complex is defined by

$$e^z = e^x(\cos y + j \sin y)$$

where $z = x + jy$ and y is measured in radians.

Mapping $z \to e^z$

- The image of the line $x = p$ is a circle, centre (0, 0), radius e^p.

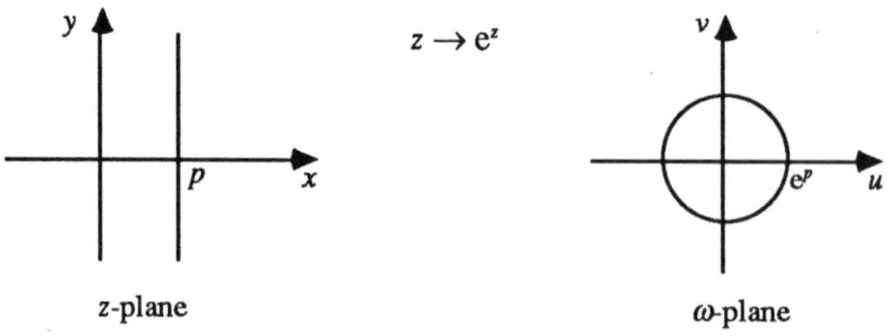

- The image of the horizontal line $y = q$ is a radial line, through the origin, with gradient tan q.

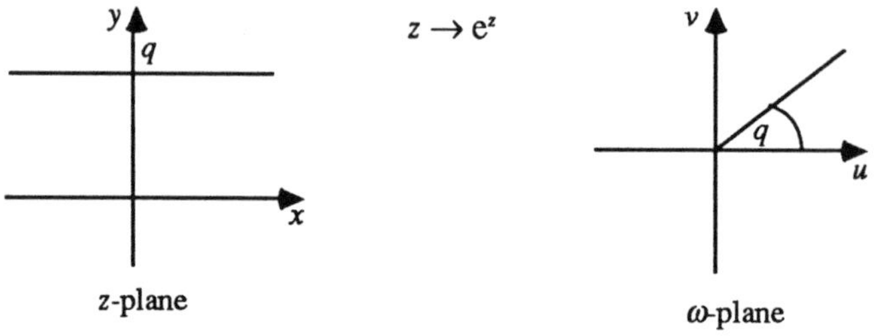

Complex powers

The definition of e^z is used to define a^z for any real number a.

$$a^z = a^x(\cos(y \ln a) + j \sin(y \ln a))$$

where $z = x + jy$.

Trigonometric functions

It is often easier to deal with the exponential function than with trigonometric functions.

Replacing $\cos x$ by $\text{Re}(e^{jx})$
$\sin x$ by $\text{Im}(e^{jx})$

can often help with calculus questions.

$$\cos z = \frac{1}{2}(e^{jz} + e^{-jz})$$

$$\sin z = \frac{1}{2j}(e^{jz} - e^{-jz})$$

$$e^{jz} = \cos z + j \sin z$$

$\ln z$

The complex logarithm of a number is **multi-valued** and defined by

$$\ln(re^{j\theta}) = \ln r + j(\theta + 2n\pi),\ n \in \mathbb{Z}$$

Using complex logarithms, a general definition of a^z can be given.

$$a^z = e^{z \ln a}, \text{ for any complex numbers } a \text{ and } z.$$

It is used in solving equations of the form $z^n = a$.

Euler's relation

$e^{j\pi} = -1$. Remarkable result which connects e, j, π and -1 in one expression.

■ Express the following in $x + jy$ form.

(a) $e^{j\frac{\pi}{4}}$ (b) 5^{2+3j}

● (a) $e^{j\frac{\pi}{4}} = \cos\frac{\pi}{4} + j\sin\frac{\pi}{4}$

$= \frac{\sqrt{2}}{2} + j\frac{\sqrt{2}}{2}$

(b) $5^{2+3j} = 5^2 \times 5^{3j}$

$= 25(\cos(3\ln 5) + j\sin(3\ln 5))$

$= 2.89 - 24.83j$

■ Express $\sqrt{3} + j$ in exponential form.

●

$\theta = \frac{\pi}{6}$ $R = 2$

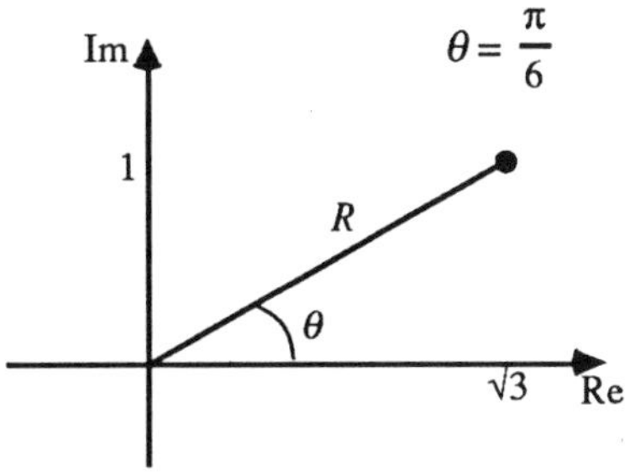

$\sqrt{3} + j = 2e^{j\frac{\pi}{6}}$

■ Find $\ln(2 - j)$ in the form $a + jb$.

● $2 - j = \sqrt{5}\,e^{-0.46j}$

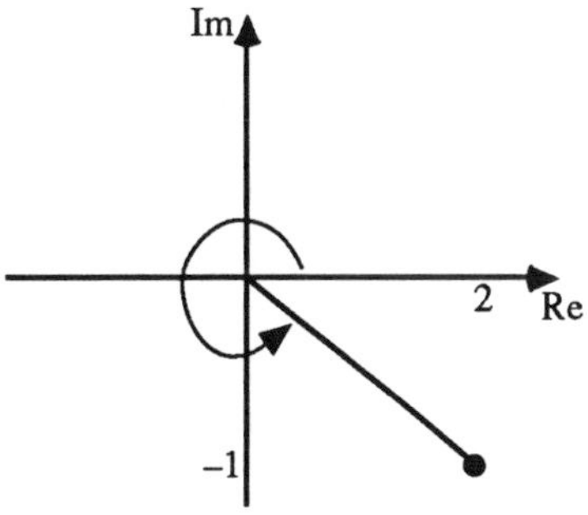

$\ln(2 - j) = \ln\sqrt{5} + j(-0.46 + 2n\pi)$

■ Find the image under the transformation $z \to e^z$ of the region bounded by the lines $x = 3$ and $y = 1$ and the coordinate axes.

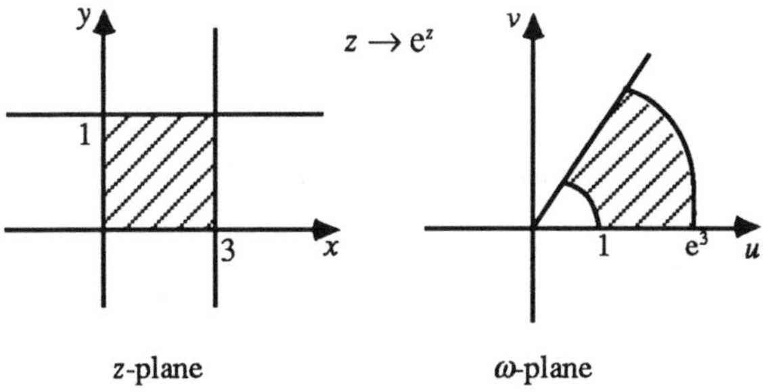

1 Express the following in $x + jy$ form:

(a) $e^{j\frac{3\pi}{4}}$

(b) 4^{-1+j}

(c) $\sin(3 - 2j)$

(d) $\ln(1 - j)$

2 Find the image under the transformation $z \to e^z$ of the region bounded by the lines $x = -4$ and $y = 2$ and the coordinate axes.

3 Plot the values of $\ln(\sqrt{3} + j)$ on an Argand diagram.

4 Use the definitions of ln to show

$$\ln\left(\frac{z_1}{z_2}\right) = \ln z_1 - \ln z_2.$$

5 Find a complex number such that $\cos z = -2$.

6 Show that the function $z \to \cos z$ maps the line $y = 1$ into an ellipse.

7 Solve the equation $z^4 = -2$.

8 Use the definitions of $\cos z$ and $\sin z$ to prove that:

(a) $\sin^2 z + \cos^2 z = 1$

(b) $\cos(t - z) = \cos t\cos z + \sin t\sin z$

9 Use the series expansion for e^x to prove that:

$$\cos z = \left(1 - \frac{z^2}{2!} + \frac{z^4}{4!} + \dots\right)$$

and

$$\sin z = \left(z - \frac{z^3}{3!} + \frac{z^5}{5!} + \dots\right)$$

10 Express in exponential form:

(a) $1 + 3j$

(b) $-1 - j$

Inversion

This transformation is given by $z \to \frac{1}{z}$. Under an inversion $[r, \theta]$ maps onto $[\frac{1}{r}, -\theta]$. For example, $[2, \frac{\pi}{2}] \to [\frac{1}{2}, -\frac{\pi}{2}]$. Also:

- Straight lines through the origin map onto straight lines through the origin, all other straight lines mapping to circles through the origin.
- All circles through the origin map onto straight lines, all other circles mapping to circles.

Combined transformations

Some transformations are combinations of an inversion and other transformations. For example, $z \to \frac{2}{z+3}$ is a combination of three transformations:

(i) a translation of $\begin{bmatrix} 3 \\ 0 \end{bmatrix}$

(ii) an inversion

(iii) an enlargement of factor 2

in that order.

Similarly, $z \to \frac{j}{2z}$ is:

(i) an enlargement by factor 2

(ii) an inversion

(iii) a 90° anti-clockwise rotation about the origin

(Note that (i) and (ii) could be reversed.)

Linear transformations

Transformations of the form $z \to \frac{az+b}{cz+d}$ are called linear transformations and can also be expressed as a combination of simple transformations. Such transformations can be reduced to the form $z \to \alpha + \frac{\beta}{z+\gamma}$.

For example, $\frac{3z+j}{z-j} = \frac{3(z-j)+4j}{z-j} = 3 + \frac{4j}{z-j}$ so $z \to \frac{3z+j}{z-j}$ is equivalent to $z \to 3 + \frac{4j}{z-j}$. The linear transformation here is:

(i) a translation $\begin{bmatrix} 0 \\ -1 \end{bmatrix}$

(ii) an inversion

(iii) an enlargement factor 4

(iv) a 90° anti-clockwise rotation

(v) a translation $\begin{bmatrix} 3 \\ 0 \end{bmatrix}$

(Note that α, β, γ above are complex numbers.)

The Joukowski transformation

This is defined by the transformation $z \to z + \frac{1}{z}$, and has important applications in the study of lines of flow around an obstruction.

■ Find the image of $\arg(z-1)=\frac{\pi}{2}$ under $z \to \frac{1}{z}$.

● You have:

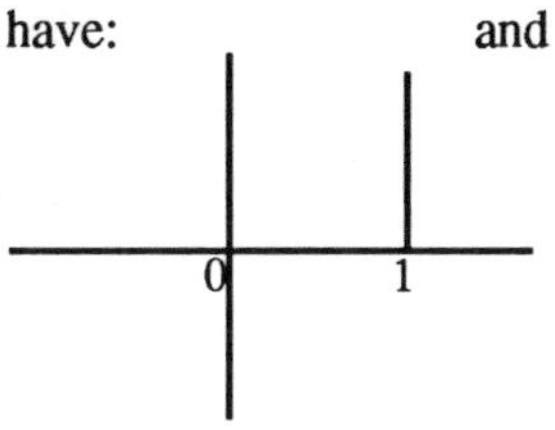

and $1 \to 1$
$\infty \to 0$
$1+j \to \frac{1}{2}(1-j)$

Since you know the half line maps onto a semi-circle the image is:

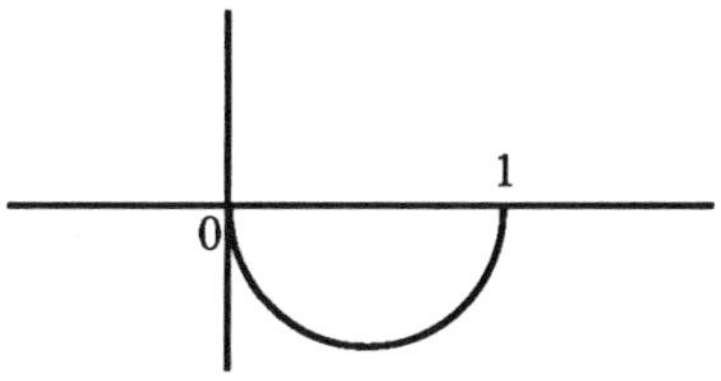

■ Use an algebraic method to find the locus of ω when $\omega = \frac{2}{z+1}$ and $|z| = 1$.

● $\omega = \frac{2}{z+1} \Rightarrow z = \frac{2}{\omega} - 1 = \frac{2-\omega}{\omega}$

$\Rightarrow \left|\frac{2-\omega}{\omega}\right| = 1$

$\Rightarrow |2-\omega| = |\omega|$

$\Rightarrow |\omega - 2| = |\omega|$

This is the perpendicular bisector of (0, 0), (2, 0) which is the line $u = 1$.

■ By expressing the transformation $z \to \frac{4z+3j}{2z+j}$ as a series of transformations find the image of

$$|z+2j| = 1$$

● $\frac{4z+3j}{2z+j} = \frac{2(2z+j)+j}{2z+j} = 2 + \frac{j}{2z+j}$ then

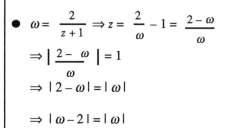

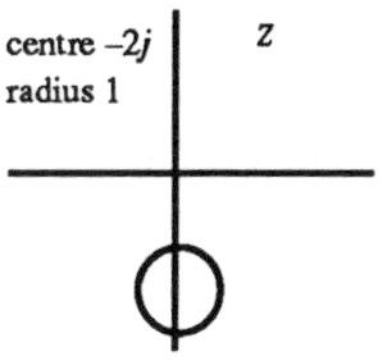

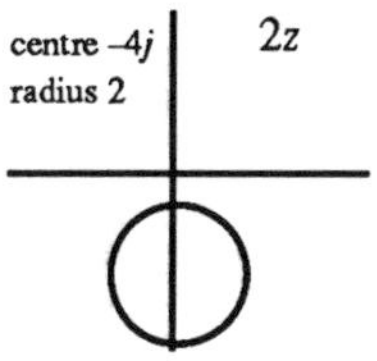

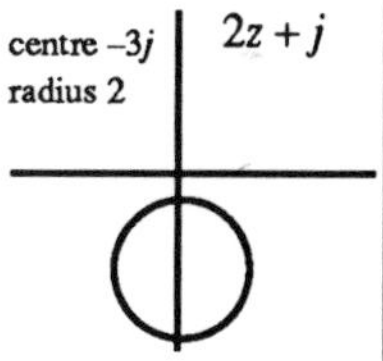

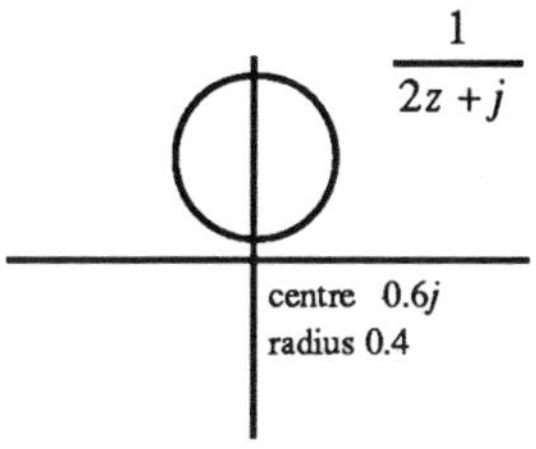

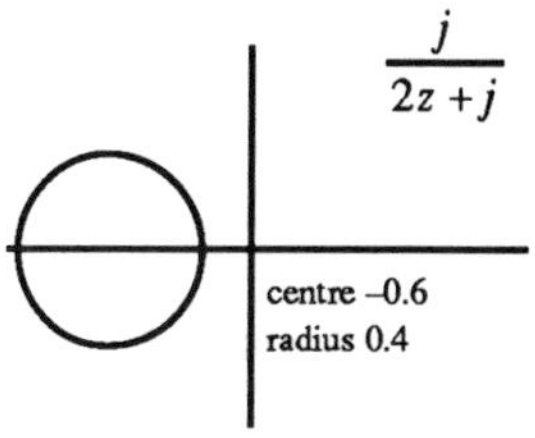

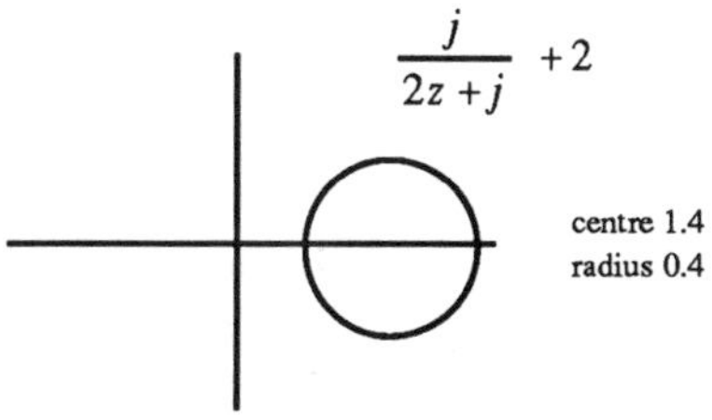

The equation is $|z - \frac{7}{5}| = \frac{2}{5}$.

1 Find the image of $\pm j$ under the transformations:

(a) $\omega = \frac{1}{z}$ (b) $\omega = \frac{\frac{2}{z}}{z+1}$

2 Sketch the locus of the line $x = 1$ under the transformation $\omega = \frac{1}{z+1}$.

3 Find the image of $|z - j| = 1$ under $z \to \frac{z+1}{z}$.

4 Use an algebraic method to transform $|z-1| = 1$ with $z \to \frac{2}{2z+1}$.

5 Express in the form $\alpha + \frac{\beta}{z+\gamma}$:

(a) $\frac{z+5}{z-2}$ (b) $\frac{2z+1}{z-2}$

(c) $\frac{z-1}{2z+1}$ (d) $\frac{jz+3j+2}{z+3}$

6 Describe the transformation in 5(d) above as a combination of four transformations.

7 Find the image in the ω-plane of $|z| = 1$ given $\omega = \frac{z+1}{z+2}$.

8 (a) Find the image of four points on the circle $|z| = 1$ under the Joukowski transformation.

(b) By writing $z + \frac{1}{z}$ as a single fraction show that the maximum value of $|z + \frac{1}{z}|$ is 2 for this circle.

9 Find the image of:

(a) $|z - j| = 1$ under $z \to \frac{2}{z^*}$

(b) $\arg(z-1) = \frac{\pi}{3}$ under $z \to \frac{2z+1}{z-1}$

Orbits

A **recurrence relation** (i.e. an iterative equation) which defines z_{n+1} in terms of z_n is called a **dynamical system.** Given a starting value z_0, the values z_1, z_2 etc. can then be found and this sequence of values is called an **orbit**. Recurrence relations of the form $z_{n+1} = cz_n + d$ define **linear** dynamical systems.

For example, given the non-linear dynamical system

$$z_{n+1} = z_n^2 + 1 \text{ and } z_0 = 1 + j$$

then $\quad z_1 = (1 + j)^2 + 1 = 1 + 2j$

and $\quad z_2 = (1 + 2j)^2 + 1 = -2 + 4j$

etc.

The points thus obtained $z_0, z_1, z_2, \ldots$ (the orbit) can be plotted on an Argand diagram and joined:

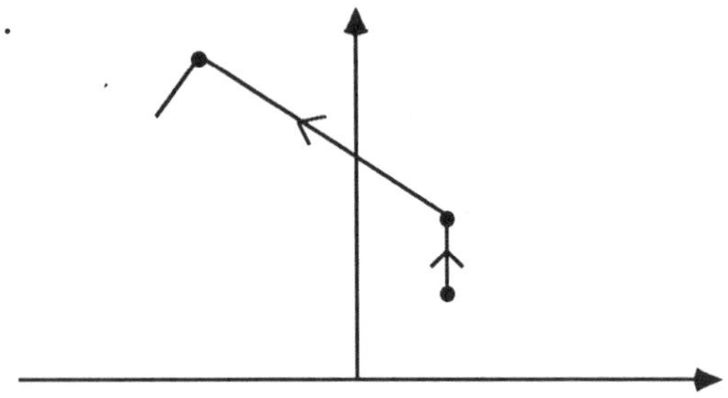

Various types of orbit can follow from a particular recurrence relation and starting point. The orbit may

- converge on a particular point, called an attractor;
- diverge from a particular point, called a repeller;
- go to a series of points before returning to its starting point. If there are n different points visited, it is periodic with order n. The orbit may oscillate between 2 points or just keep repeating the same value – in this last case the point is called a **fixed point**.

Other orbital situations may occur but these are the main ones.

It is useful to remember and apply the properties of complex number arithmetic. For example, given $z_{n+1} = 2jz_n$, since $2j = [2, 90°]$ in modulus-argument form, successive points in the orbit will have their modulus multiplied by 2 and their argument increased by 90°. So the orbit can be drawn (starting with $z_0 = 1$ say) without going through the calculations:

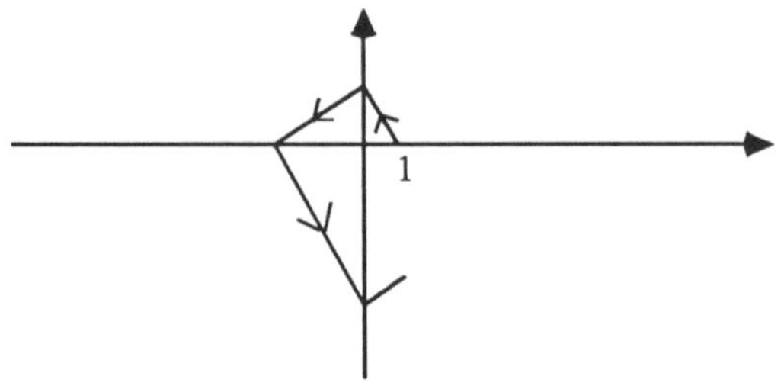

Julia and Mandelbrot sets

These are both based on the recurrence relation $z_{n+1} = z_n^2 + c$. There are an infinite number of Julia sets (depending on c) but only one Mandelbrot set.

A particular Julia set is defined by a specific value for c, for example, $z_{n+1} = z_n^2 + 1 + j$. Then each point in the Argand plane is taken as a starting point, z_0, of the iteration. That point will either go to infinity or not. The Julia set is the set of all these points whose orbits do not tend to infinity.

For the Mandelbrot set each point in the Argand plane is put as c in $z_{n+1} = z_n^2 + c$, the starting point always being $z_0 = 0$. Again, the set of points which do not tend to infinity is the Mandelbrot set.

■ Describe the orbit given by the recurrence relation:

$$z_{n+1} = jz_n^2 - 1 \text{ and } z_0 = 0$$

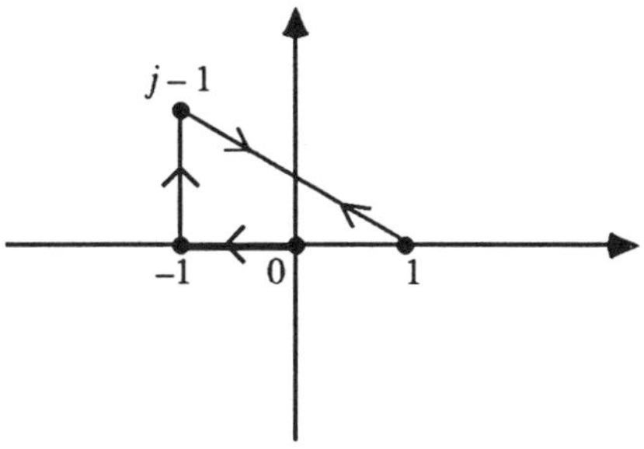

● $z_1 = -1$
$z_2 = j - 1$
$z_3 = 1$
$z_4 = j - 1$

So after going through 0 and –1 the orbit settles into an oscillation between the points 1 and $j - 1$.

The period is 2.

■ Find the value of c so that

$$z_{n+1} = cz_n + j$$

starting with $z_0 = 0$ is periodic with period 2.

● If the period is 2, then 2 iterations should give the initial value 0:

$z_1 = j$
$z_2 = cj + j = 0$
$c = -1$

■ Find the fixed points in the dynamical system:

$$z_{n+1} = 2z_n - jz_n^2 - 6j$$

● The fixed points iterate onto themselves so they are the solutions to $z = 2z - jz^2 - 6j$

$$\Rightarrow \quad jz^2 - z + 6j = 0$$

$$\Rightarrow \quad z^2 + jz + 6 = 0$$

$$\Rightarrow \quad z = \frac{-j \pm \sqrt{(-1 - 24)}}{2}$$

$$= \frac{-j \pm 5j}{2}$$

$$= 2j, -3j$$

1 Generate the first 4 terms of the sequence defined by $z_{n+1} = jz_n + j$ and $z_0 = 1$.

2 Find any fixed points for the systems defined by

(a) $z_{n+1} = 3z_n - 2$

(b) $z_{n+1} = z_n^2$

(c) $z_{n+1} = z_n^2 - 6$

(d) $z_{n+1} = jz_n^2 + 2j$

3 Show that $z_0 = 1 + j$ is periodic in the system

$$z_{n+1} = jz_n + 1$$

and give the order of its period.

4 Give a dynamical system in which all non-zero points are periodic of order 5.

5 Find a point in the Julia set

$$z_{n+1} = z_n^2 - 6$$

6 Show that –2 is in the Mandelbrot set but 2 is not.

7 If $z_{n+1} = az_n^2 + z_n$ and $z_0 = j$, find z_1 and z_2.

8 Find a value of c such that $z_0 = j$ is periodic of order 2 in the dynamical system

$$z_{n+1} = jz_n^2 + c$$

9 A dynamical system is defined by

$$z_{n+1} = az_n^2 + b$$

where a and b are complex numbers.

Given that the orbit of $z_0 = 0$ is shown in the diagram below, find the values of a and b and confirm that the period is of order 2.

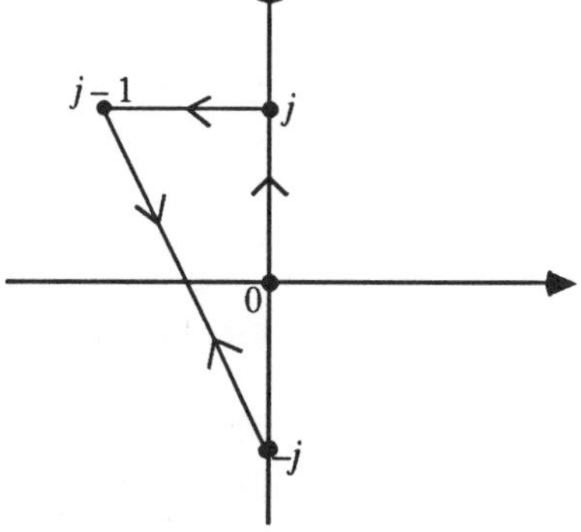

NUMERICAL METHODS

Adding errors

Measurements are not exact and can be written in the form $a \pm e$.

If measurements are **added or subtracted** the errors are **added.**

$$(a \pm e) + (b \pm f) = (a + b) \pm (e + f)$$

and also:

$$(a \pm e) - (b \pm f) = (a - b) \pm (e + f)$$

The combination of errors can be important when calculating areas by numerical methods. If an area is calculated using 10^5 strips and the area of each strip is known with an accuracy of 10^{-6}, the possible total error is $10^5 \times 10^{-6} = 0.1$.

It may be better to use a smaller number of strips, even though the area of each strip is known to a lower degree of accuracy.

Relative errors

$a \pm e = a\,(1 \pm \frac{e}{a})$. $\frac{e}{a}$ is the **relative error**, abbreviated to r.

So $a \pm e$ can be written as $a\,(1 \pm r)$.

When **multiplying or dividing**, the relative errors are **added.**

$$a(1 \pm r) \times b(1 \pm s) \approx ab(1 \pm (r + s))$$

and also:

$$a(1 \pm r) \div b(1 \pm s) \approx \frac{a}{b}(1 \pm (r + s))$$

Binary form

Binary form means base 2.

The column headings are:

$\ldots\ 2^3\ 2^2\ 2^1\ 2^0\ 2^{-1}\ 2^{-2}\ 2^{-3} \ldots$

10011.101_2 is equal to:

$$16 + 2 + 1 + \frac{1}{2} + \frac{1}{8} = 19\frac{5}{8}$$

Storing numbers

Numbers are stored in calculators in **floating point notation.**

This means they are written in the form $a \times 2^b$, where $0.1_2 \leq a \leq 1_2$ and b is an integer.

$$0.101 \times 2^5 = (\frac{1}{2} + \frac{1}{8}) \times 32 = 20$$

$$7 = \frac{7}{8} \times 8 = 0.111_2 \times 2^3$$

a is called the **mantissa** and b is called the **exponent.**

Many numbers cannot be stored accurately, since simple decimals do not always have simple binary representations. For example:

0.3 in binary is 0.0100110011001 ...

(See the page opposite for this conversion.)

This process can occasionally lead to serious, or **catastrophic** errors, particularly when the calculator is used to add or subtract numbers of very different sizes or to divide by a very small number.

■ $y = (1.03 + 1.13)(4.26 - 3.87)$

What is the maximum error in y if each number is correct to ± 0.01?

● $y = (2.16 \pm 0.02)(0.39 \pm 0.02)$
$= 2.16(1 \pm 0.009) \times 0.39(1 \pm 0.051)$
$= 0.84(1 \pm 0.06) = 0.84 \pm 0.05$

The maximum error is 0.05 (to 1 s.f.)

■ x has a relative error of 0.04.

What are the percentage errors for (a) x^2 and (b) $\sqrt{x}$?

● (a) $0.04 + 0.04 = 0.08$, so 8%

(b) Squaring doubles the percentage error, so square rooting will halve it. The percentage error for $\sqrt{x}$ is 2%.

■ Write 0.3 in binary form, using the process of successive doubling.

● $0.3 \times 2 = 0.6$, or $\underline{0} + 0.6$ — 1st digit is $\underline{0}$

$0.6 \times 2 = 1.2$, or $\underline{1} + 0.2$ — 2nd digit is $\underline{1}$

$0.2 \times 2 = 0.4$, or $\underline{0} + 0.4$ — 3rd digit is $\underline{0}$

$0.4 \times 2 = 0.8$, or $\underline{0} + 0.8$ — 4th digit is $\underline{0}$

$0.8 \times 2 = 1.6$, or $\underline{1} + 0.6$ — 5th digit is $\underline{1}$

$0.6 \times 2 = 1.2$, or $\underline{1} + 0.2$ — 6th digit is $\underline{1}$

There is clearly a repeating cycle.

The decimal 0.3 in binary is

0.0100110011001 ...

1 What is the maximum relative error for

$$\left(\frac{2.16 \times 1.24}{3.08}\right)^2$$

if each number is correct to:

(a) ± 0.01 (b) ± 0.02 (c) ± 0.005

2 The value of g can be found from the formula

$$g = \frac{4\pi^2 l}{t^2}$$

where t is the time (in seconds) for 1 swing of a pendulum with a string of length l m. t can be measured to $\pm$ 0.1 seconds and l is accurate to the nearest 0.5 cm.

(a) If $l = 0.5$ m and 1 swing is timed to take 1.4 seconds, find the minimum and maximum possible values of g.

(b) What is the range of values for g if 10 swings are timed to take 14.2 seconds?

3

$$d = \sqrt[3]{\left(\frac{R^2 g}{w^2}\right)}$$

where $g = 9.81$, $R = 6.36 \times 10^2$ and $w = 2.60 \times 10^{-6}$.

(a) Estimate d to 3 significant figures.

(b) What is the approximate maximum possible percentage error in d if R, g and w are correct to 3 significant figures?

4

$$A = \left(\frac{bc}{\sqrt{d}}\right)^3$$

If $b = 3.1 \times 10^3$, $c = 2.4 \times 10^{-8}$ and $d = 41$, all correct to 2 s.f., what is the maximum possible percentage error in the value of A?

5 (a) Change (i) 39 and (ii) 4.1 to binary.

(b) Write the number 13 in binary using floating point notation.

6 An area was estimated by dividing it into 100 strips, the area of each strip being known to an accuracy of $\pm 10^{-3}$. The area was then divided into 10 000 strips, the area of each strip being known to an accuracy of $\pm b$.

What can you say about the value of b if using the larger number of strips gave a more accurate answer for the total area?

7 A student estimated the gradient of $y = e^x$ at $x = 1$ by calculating

$$\frac{(e^{1+h} - e^1)}{h}$$

for $h = 10^{-5}$ and then $h = 10^{-6}$, but her calculator only worked to 8 significant figures.

(a) Give her first answer in the form $b \pm f$ and check that the actual value of the gradient of the curve at $x = 1$ is included in this range.

(b) Work out her second answer and explain why the smaller value of h did not give a better estimate.

Estimating area

There are various sensible ways of calculating the area under a graph. Some of these are illustrated for the function $f(x) = \sin x$ for $x = 0$ to 2 (radians!) with 4 strips.

First ordinate rule

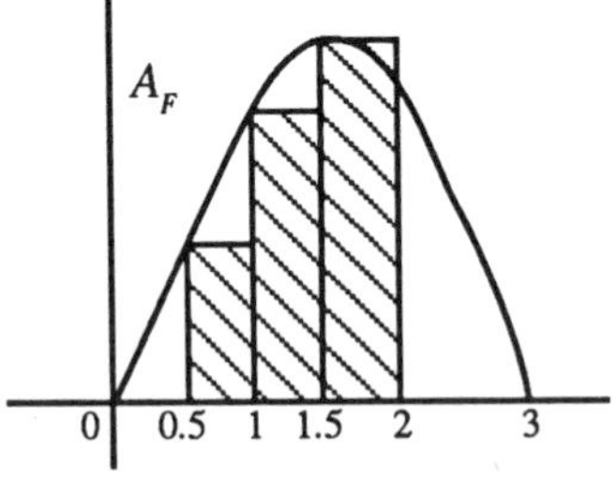

$A_F = 0.5 \sin 0 + 0.5 \sin 0.5$
$+ 0.5 \sin 1 + 0.5 \sin 1.5$
$= 1.159$

Last ordinate rule

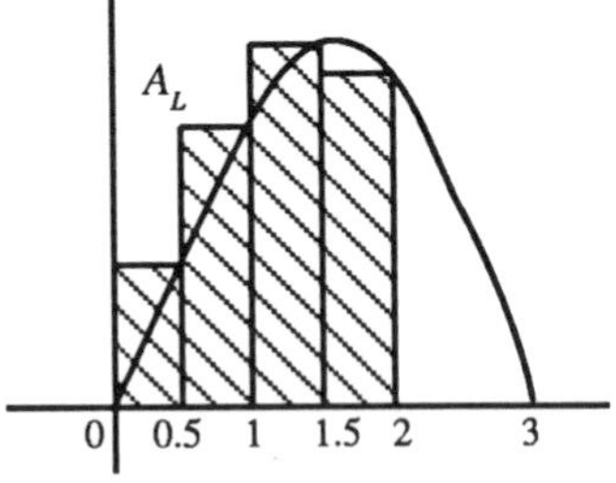

$A_L = 0.5 \sin 0.5 + 0.5 \sin 1$
$+ 0.5 \sin 1.5 + 0.5 \sin 2$
$= 1.614$

Trapezium rule

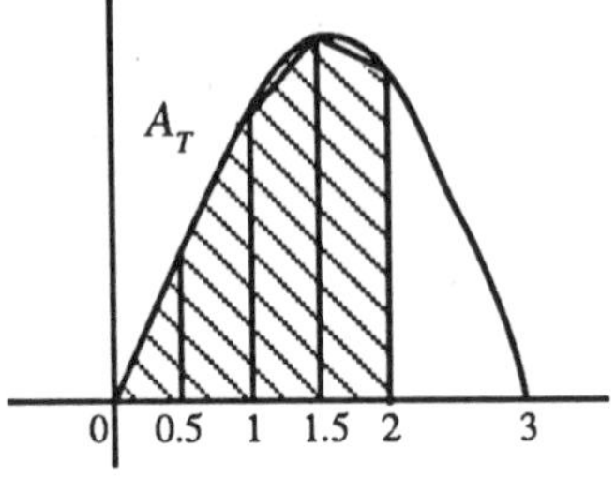

$A_T = \frac{1}{2} \times 0.5 (\sin 0 + \sin 0.5) \ldots$
$+ \frac{1}{2} \times 0.5 (\sin 1.5 + \sin 2)$
$= 1.387$

Mid-ordinate rule

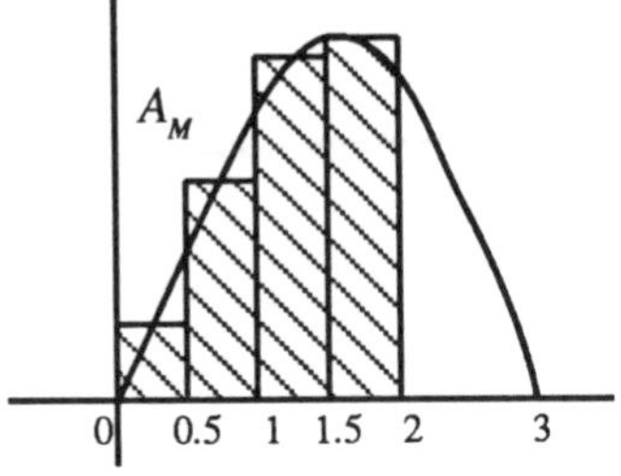

$A_M = 0.5 \sin 0.25 + 0.5 \sin 0.75$
$+ 0.5 \sin 1.25 + 0.5 \sin 1.75$
$= 1.431$

In each case the strip width for 4 strips is $\frac{2-0}{4} = 0.5$ Note that $A_T = \frac{1}{2}(A_F + A_L)$, the average of these two estimates.

Order of estimates

In the first and last ordinate rules doubling the number of strips halves the errors thus doubling the accuracy. Multiplying the number of strips by r reduces the errors by a factor of $\frac{1}{r}$. This is called a **first order** approximation.

In the trapezium and mid-ordinate rules, doubling the number of strips reduces the error by a factor of $4 = 2^2$. Multiplying the number of strips by r reduces the error by a factor of $\frac{1}{r^2}$. This is called a **second order** approximation. In general, in an nth order approximation, multiplying the number of strips by r reduces the error by a factor of $\frac{1}{r^n}$.

Simpson's rule

For an increasing function (or part of a function) with decreasing gradient, the trapezium rule plainly under estimates the area. The mid-ordinate rule overstates the area. For other functions this is either exactly the same or exactly opposite.

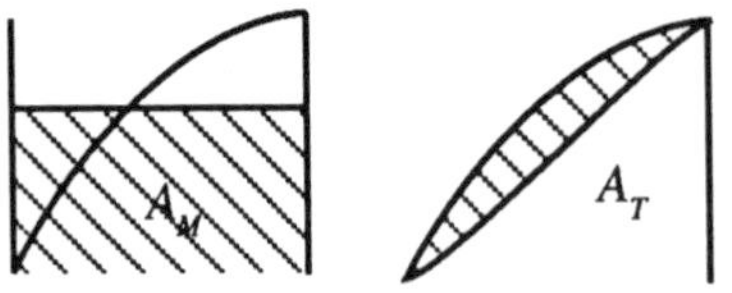

On average the mid-ordinate rule is **twice** as accurate as the trapezium rule. Simpson's rule is defined as $A_S = \frac{2}{3} A_M + \frac{1}{3} A_T$. It can be calculated by this method or directly from the formula in the formula book.

Order of Simpson's approximation

You would expect Simpson's rule to be more accurate than mid-ordinate or trapezium method. In fact, Simpson's rule is of order 4 so increasing the number of strips by a factor of r increases the accuracy by a factor $\frac{1}{r^4}$.

Exact answers

For constant functions A_F and A_L are exact, they are of order 1 so errors occur in the x^1 term. For linear functions A_M and A_T are exact: they are of order 2 so errors occur in the x^2 term. A_S is exact for cubic functions: it is of order 4 so errors occur in the x^4 term.

■ (a) Calculate an estimate for $\int_4^{12} e^{x/4}dx$ using Simpson's rule with (i) 4 strips (ii) 2 strips.

(b) Use algebraic integration to obtain the true answer and the errors in your estimates.

(c) Verify that Simpson's rule is a fourth order estimate.

● (a) (i) $h = \frac{12-4}{4} = 2$, so $x_0 = 4, x_1 = 6, x_2 = 8, x_3 = 10, x_4 = 12$.

x_i	4	6	8	10	12
$f(x_i)$	e^1	$e^{1.5}$	e^2	$e^{2.5}$	e^3

$$A_S = \frac{1}{3}h[f_0 + f_n + 4(f_1 + f_3 + \ldots) + 2(f_2 + f_4 + \ldots)]$$
$$= \frac{1}{3}\times 2 \times [e^1 + e^3 + 4(e^{1.5} + e^{2.5}) + 2e^2]$$
$$= 69.492442$$

(ii) $h = \frac{12-4}{2} = 4$, so $x_0 = 4, x_1 = 8, x_2 = 12$.

$$A_S = \frac{1}{3}\times 4 \times [e^1 + e^3 + 4e^2] = 69.81391$$

(b) $\int_4^{12} e^{x/4}\,dx = [4e^{x/4}]_4^{12} = 4(e^3 - e^1) = 69.46902$

Error in (i) = 0.02342
Error in (ii) = 0.34489

(c) Error in (ii) ÷ error in (i) ≈ 14.7 ≈ 16.
So dividing the strip width by 2 divides errors by 2^4. Therefore Simpson's rule is of order 4.

■ Calculate an estimate for $\int_1^4 \frac{x}{1+x^2}\,dx$ correct to 4 decimal places using Simpson's rule with 6 strips. Use integration to find the exact value of this integral as a logarithm. Find the percentage error in your estimate.

● $h = \frac{4-1}{6} = 0.5$, $f_0 = f(1) = \frac{1}{1+1^2} = 0.5$

$$f_1 = f(1.5) = \frac{1.5}{1+1.5^2} = 0.46154$$

and so on.

$$A_S = \frac{1}{3}\times 0.5 \times [0.5 + 0.23529 + 4(0.46154 + 0.34483 + 0.26415) + 2(0.4 + 0.3)]$$
$$= 1.06956$$

By direct integration since $\frac{d}{dx}(1 + x^2) = 2x$:

$$\int_1^4 \frac{x}{1+x^2}\,dx = \frac{1}{2}\int_1^4 \frac{2x\,dx}{1+x^2} = \left[\frac{1}{2}\ln|1+x^2|\right]_1^4$$

$\frac{1}{2}\ln 17 - \frac{1}{2}\ln 2 = \frac{1}{2}\ln 8.5 = 1.07003$ (to 5 d.p.)

Error = 1.07003 – 1.06956 = 4.7×10^{-4}

Percentage error = $\frac{4.7\times 10^{-4}}{1.07003} \times 100 = 0.044\%$

1 Use Simpson's rule with 8 strips to find an estimate for $\int_0^1 e^{2x}\,dx$. Use integration to find the exact value of this integral and hence find the percentage error in your estimate.

2 A Christmas decoration is obtained by rotating the curve $y = 10\sin x$ for values of x between $x = 0$ and $x = \frac{\pi}{2}$, about the x-axis by 2π radians (all dimensions in cm). Use Simpson's rule with 4 strips to find the volume of this decoration. Check your answer by direct integration.

3 Calculate the exact value of the Simpson's rule estimate for $\int_0^2 x^3\,dx$ using 4 strips. Evaluate the integral directly and verify that Simpson's rule gives an exactly correct value for this integral.

4 A vase is made by rotating $y = e^x$ between $x = 0$ and $x = 1$ about the y-axis for 2π radians. Show that the volume inside the vase is given by $V = \pi\int_1^e (\ln y)^2\,dy$ and calculate an approximate value for this volume using Simpson's rule with 6 strips.

5 Let A_F, A_L, A_M and A_T be the first ordinate, last ordinate, mid-ordinate and trapezium rule estimate for $\int_0^1 e^{x^2}dx$ based on 4 strips. Calculate A_F, A_L, A_M and A_T.

(a) Check that $A_T = \frac{1}{2}(A_F + A_L)$.

(b) Check that $A_F < A_M < A_L$.

(c) Verify that the Simpson's rule estimate A_s based on 8 strips satisfies $A_s = \frac{2A_M + A_T}{3}$

6 Calculate Simpson's rule estimates for $\int_0^1 e^x\,dx$ based on 2, 4 and 8 strips. Use integration to obtain an exact value for this integral. By calculating errors in your estimate show that Simpson's rule is a fourth order method.

7 The braking force on a car during a time interval of 6 seconds is given below.

t (s)	0	1	2	3	4	5	6
F (N)	0	400	800	1100	1400	1600	1700

Use Simpson's rule to calculate an estimate for $\int_0^6 F\,dt$ which is the loss in momentum of the car.

Estimating gradients numerically

The gradient of $y = f(x)$ at the point $(a, f(a))$ can be approximated by the gradient of the chord which connects the point $(a, f(a))$ to another point $((a + h), f(a + h))$ on $y = f(x)$, where h is small.

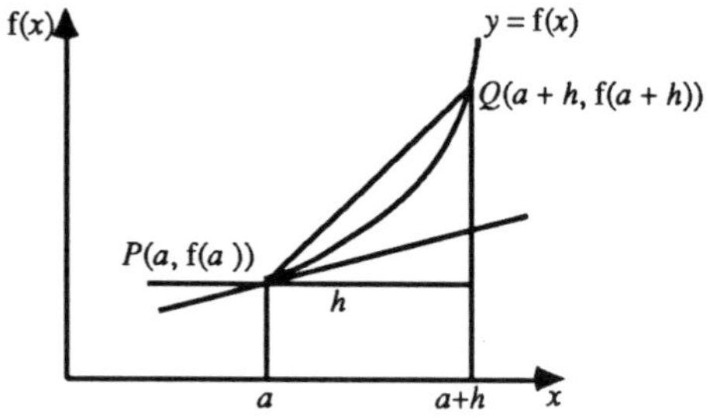

$$\text{Gradient of chord} = \frac{f(a+h) - f(a)}{h} \approx f'(x)$$

Another approximation to the gradient of $y = f(x)$ is given by:

$$\frac{f(a+h) - f(a-h)}{2h}$$

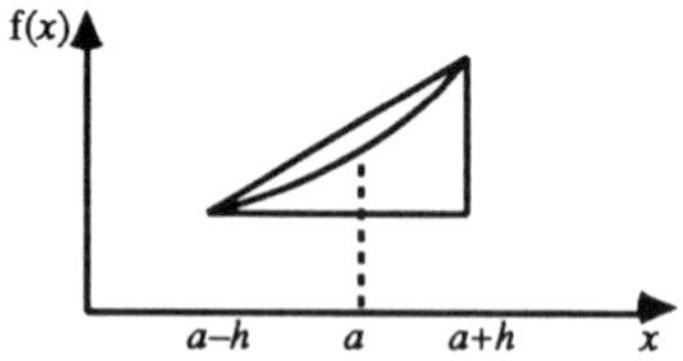

Absolute error

This is equal to [estimated value – actual value].

Taylor approximations

These give approximations for $f(a + h)$ when $f(a)$ and its differentials are known. **Taylor's first approximation** to $f(x)$, centred on $x = a$, is given by:

$$f(a + h) \approx f(a) + f'(a)h$$

This is obviously not very good when the graph is very curved at the point where $x = a$.

Taylor's second approximation to a function $f(x)$ at $x = a$ is

$$f(a + h) \approx f(a) + f'(a)h + f''(a)\frac{h^2}{2}$$

Higher degree polynomials

Taylor's rth approximation (like the first and second), is a polynomial of degree r.

When centred on $x = a$,

$$f(a + h) \approx f(a) + hf'(a) + h^2\frac{f''(a)}{2!} + \ldots + h^r\frac{f^r(a)}{r!} \text{ where } h \text{ is small.}$$

When centred on $x = 0$,

$$f(h) \approx f(0) + hf'(0) + h^2\frac{f''(0)}{2!} + \ldots + h^r\frac{f^r(0)}{r!}$$

This is normally known as a Maclaurin polynomial.

Error in a Taylor approximation

The error in a Taylor approximation of degree r centred on $x = 0$ is proportional to x^{r+1} for small values of x.

Taylor series

The infinite series given by

$$f(a) + (x - a)f'(a) + (x - a)^2\frac{f''(a)}{2!} + \ldots + (x - a)^r\frac{f^r(a)}{r!} + \ldots$$

is called the Taylor series for the function $f(x)$.

When this is written for the case $a = 0$, it is usually referred to as the **Maclaurin series.**

$$f(0) + f'(0)\,x + f''(0)\frac{x^2}{2!} + f^{(3)}(0)\frac{x^3}{3!} + \ldots + f^r(0)\frac{x^r}{r!} + \ldots$$

The radius of convergence is the range of values of x for which the Taylor series (or Maclaurin series) converges to $f(x)$.

■ Derive Taylor's second approximation to $e^{\sin x}$ centred on $x = 0$. Use this to find an approximate value for $e^{\sin(0.2)}$. Calculate the absolute error.

● $f(x) = e^{\sin x} \Rightarrow f(0) = e^{\sin(0)} = 1$

$f'(x) = (\cos x)e^{\sin x} = (\cos x)f(x) \Rightarrow f'(0) = \cos(0)f(0) = 1$

$f''(x) = (\cos x)f'(x) + (-\sin x)f(x) \Rightarrow f''(0) = 1$

Taylor's second approximation to $e^{\sin x}$ is given by:

$$e^{\sin x} \approx f(0) + f'(0)x + f''(0)\frac{x^2}{2!} = 1 + x + \frac{x^2}{2}$$

$$e^{\sin(0.2)} \approx 1 + (0.2) + \frac{(0.2)^2}{2} \approx 1.22$$

The actual value of $e^{\sin(0.2)}$ is 1.2198.

The absolute error = 1.22 – 1.2198 = 0.0002

■ Find the Taylor series, centred on $x = 0$, for $f(x) = \ln(1 + ax)$, for $a > 0$. State the range of values of x for which the series is valid (i.e. the radius of convergence). Hence write down the series for $g(x) = \ln(1 - 2x)$ as far as the term in x^5. Find g(0.2), using your series correct to 2 decimal places.

● $f(x) = \ln(1 + ax) \Rightarrow f(0) = \ln 1 = 0$

$$f'(x) = \frac{a}{1 + ax} \Rightarrow f'(0) = a$$

$$f''(x) = \frac{-a^2}{(1 + ax)^2} \Rightarrow f''(0) = -a^2$$

$$f^{(3)}(x) = \frac{2a^3}{(1 + ax)^3} \Rightarrow f^{(3)}(0) = 2a^3$$

$$f^{(4)}(x) = \frac{-6a^4}{(1 + ax)^4} \Rightarrow f^{(4)}(0) = -6a^4$$

$$f^{(5)}(x) = \frac{24a^5}{(1 + ax)^5} \Rightarrow f^{(5)}(0) = 24a^5$$

$$f(x) = f(0) + f'(0)x + f''(0)\frac{x^2}{2!} + f^{(3)}(0)\frac{x^3}{3!} \ldots$$

$$\ln(1 + ax) = ax - a^2\frac{x^2}{2} + 2a^3\frac{x^3}{6} - 6a^4\frac{x^4}{24} + 24a^5\frac{x^5}{120}$$

$$= ax - \frac{a^2x^2}{2} + \frac{a^3x^3}{3} - \frac{a^4x^4}{4} + \frac{a^5x^5}{5} \ldots$$

Radius of convergence: $-1 < ax \leq 1$

$$\Rightarrow \quad -\frac{1}{a} < x \leq \frac{1}{a}$$

Letting $a = 2$ and replacing x by $-x$ in the series for $\ln(1 + ax)$, gives:

$$g(x) = \ln(1 - 2x) \approx -2x - 2x^2 - \frac{8x^3}{3} - 4x^4 - \frac{32x^5}{5}$$

Radius of convergence:

$$(-1 < -2x \leq 1) \Rightarrow (-0.5 \leq x < 0.5)$$

$g(0.2) = \ln(0.6)$

$$\approx -2(0.2) - 2(0.2)^2 - \frac{8(0.2)^3}{3} - 4(0.2)^4 - \frac{32(0.2)^5}{5}$$

≈ -0.51 (2 decimal places)

1 Estimate the gradient of the graph of $y = e^{\sin x}$ at $x = 2$,

(a) using the first approximation, with $h = 0.1$;

(b) using the second approximation with $h = 0.1$.

Consider the absolute error for each method for $h = 0.1$, 0.01 and 0.001. What can you say about the order of accuracy of each method?

2 Find Taylor's second approximation to $f(x) = e^x$ centred on $x = 1$.

Use your graphical calculator to draw the graphs of $y = e^x$ and $y = \frac{e}{2}(x^2 + 1)$ superimposed.

What does this tell you about Taylor's second approximation? Is it 'better' than Taylor's first approximation?

3 Show that the Taylor polynomial of degree 5 for the function $S(x) = \sin x$ is

$$s(x) = x - \frac{1}{6}x^3 + \frac{1}{120}x^5$$

Use your graphical calculator to draw the graphs of S(x) and s(x) on the same axes for values of x in the range $-\pi < x < \pi$.

Comment on what this shows about s(x) as an approximation to S(x).

4 Write down the Taylor's series for $\cos x$, centred on $x = 0$.

Deduce the Taylor's series for $\cos 3x$ and state the range of values for x for which this series is valid.

Use your graphical calculator to compare the 10th polynomial approximation to $\cos 3x$ with the graph of $y = \cos 3x$.

5 For $y = e^{x^2}$, show that $y^{(3)} = 2(2y' + xy'')$.

By continued differentiation, or otherwise, find the Maclaurin series for y as far as the term in x^6.

Hence write down the series for e^{4x^2} in ascending powers of x.

Solving equations

First of all, locate a root approximately by finding a sign change or by using graphs. Then find a better approximation to this root by one of the methods described below.

■ Locate the real root of $x^3 - 2x^2 - 3 = 0$ between two consecutive integers.

● Call the left-hand side f(x). Then f(2) = – 3 and f(3) = 6. The change of sign indicates a root in the interval [2, 3], since f(x) is continuous.

Bisection

Repeatedly halve the interval and look for sign changes. In the example f(2.5) = + 0.125 → [2, 2.5], f(2.25) = –1.734 → [2.25, 2.5], and so on until the answer is accurate enough.

Decimal search

Work out f(x) for x = 2.1, 2.2, 2.3, ... until the sign changes. f(2.4) = – 0.696, f(2.5) = + 0.125. Now take x = 2.41, 2.42, 2.43, ... until the sign changes. Continue until the answer is accurate enough.

x = g(x) iteration

Rearrange the equation so that x appears alone on the left-hand side.

For example, $x^3 = 2x^2 + 3$, leading to $x = \sqrt[3]{(2x^2 + 3)}$, giving $x_{n+1} = \sqrt[3]{(2x_n^2 + 3)}$.

Choose a suitable x_1 and generate a sequence which may converge to the root. The sequence can be shown on a staircase or cobweb diagram. Draw graphs of $y = x$ and $y = g(x)$.

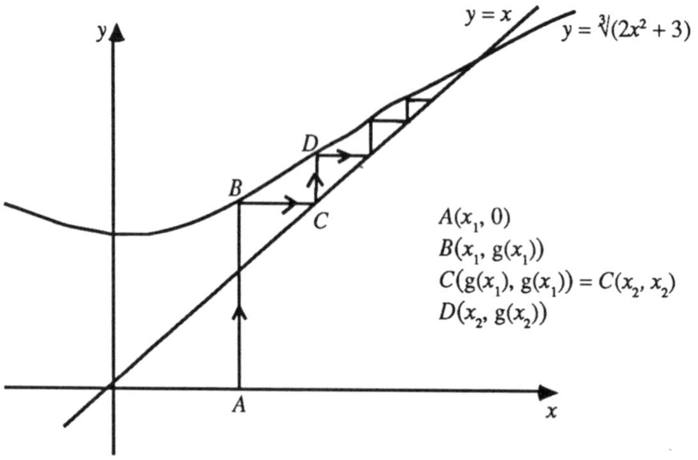

Newton-Raphson

Make sure the equation is in the form f(x) = 0, and using a suitable value for x_1 generate the sequence

$$x_{n+1} = x_n - \frac{f(x_n)}{f'(x_n)}$$

Summary

Bisection: Easy to understand and apply. n calculations reduce the interval length by a factor 2^n.

Decimal search: Easy to understand and apply. The number of calculations needed can vary greatly. It is much quicker to find 4.10 than 4.89.

x = g(x) iteration: Easy to apply, using the ANS key of a calculator. The speed of convergence depends on the value of g′ at the root. Convergence to the root $x = a$ will only occur if $|g'(a)| < 1$, and convergence is quicker for smaller values of $|g'(a)|$. Iteration is quicker than the bisection method if $|g'(a)| < \frac{1}{2}$.

Newton-Raphson: Efficient and reliable unless f′ is close to zero at the root. If f(x) is complicated, the differentiation may be tricky, but in that case the approximations $f'(x) \approx \frac{f(x+h) - f(x)}{h}$ or $f'(x) \approx \frac{f(x+h) - f(x-h)}{2h}$ can be used instead.

■ Locate the root of $e^x + x - 10 = 0$ between consecutive integers and find this root correct to 2 decimal places using:

(a) decimal search

(b) bisection

● From the graphs, there is a root near $x = 2$. If $f(x) = e^x + x - 10$, $f(2) = -0.61$, $f(3) = +13.09$. Hence [2, 3] contains the root.

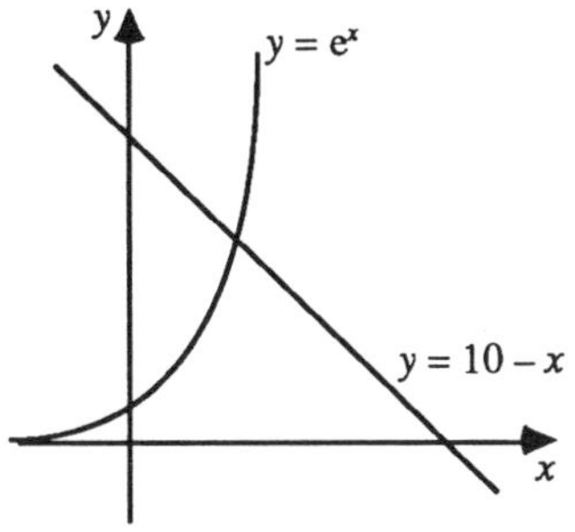

(a) $f(2.1) = +0.27 \rightarrow [2.0, 2.1]$. Find $f(2.01)$, $f(2.02)$ and so on until $f(2.07) = -0.005$,
$f(2.08) = +0.08 \rightarrow [2.07, 2.08]$
$f(2.071) = +0.0038 \rightarrow [2.070, 2.071]$
Root ≈ 2.07 to 2 decimal places.

(b) $f(2.5) = +4.68 \rightarrow [2, 2.5]$
$f(2.25) = +1.74 \rightarrow [2, 2.25]$ and so on until
$f(2.0703125) = -0.002$ and $f(2.07421875) = +0.03$ and so the root ≈ 2.07.

■ The equation $x^3 + 4x - 10 = 0$ has a real root in [1, 2]. Comment on the efficiency of these formulas derived from the equation.

(a) $x_{n+1} = \frac{1}{4}(10 - x_n^{\,3})$ (b) $x_{n+1} = \dfrac{10}{x_n^2 + 4}$

(c) $x_{n+1} = \sqrt[3]{(10 - 4x_n)}$

● Using $x_1 = 1.5$ gives these sequences

(a) 1.5, 1.656, ..., 2.574, –1.764, ... Does not converge.

(b) 1.5, 1.6, 1.524, ... Converges slowly.

(c) 1.5, 1.587, 1.540, ... Converges more quickly than (b) to 1.557.

Note that $g'(1.557)$ is (a) –1.82 (b) –0.75 (c) –0.55.

■ Find the smallest positive root of $e^{-x} - \tan x = 0$, correct to 5 decimal places, using the Newton-Raphson method.

● From graphs of $y = e^{-x}$ and $y = \tan x$, the root is approximately 0.5.

$f(x) = e^{-x} - \tan x$, $f'(x) = -e^{-x} - \sec^2 x$

$x_{n+1} = x_n - \dfrac{f(x_n)}{f'(x_n)}$ gives the sequence 0.5, 0.5316162, 0.5313909, 0.5313909.
The root is 0.53139 to 5 decimal places.

1 Find integer bounds for the roots of:

(a) $x^3 - 5x - 1 = 0$

(b) $10x^3 - 10x + 2 = 0$

2 Without drawing a graph, show that the equation $x^3 + 2x - 5 = 0$ has only one real root, and find it, correct to 2 decimal places, by:

(a) decimal search (b) bisection

Which is more efficient?

3 Show how the formulas

(a) $x_{n+1} = \sqrt[4]{(3x_n - 1)}$

(b) $x_{n+1} = \sqrt[3]{(3 - \frac{1}{x_n})}$

can be derived from $x^4 - 3x + 1 = 0$.

Which is better for finding the larger root? Show on a graph what happens when formula (a) is used with $x_1 = 2$.

4 Solve $x = \cos x$ by: (a) iteration (b) the Newton-Raphson method, starting with $x_1 = 1$, using the full calculator display value throughout. How many iterations are needed for each method before the calculator display remains unchanged?

5 Find the smallest root of $2e^{-0.25x} = \sin x$ correct to 4 decimal places.

6 Show that the equation

$$x^3 + 0.03x^2 + 0.0003x - 0.099999 = 0$$

has a root in [0, 1]. Using the Newton-Raphson method with $x_1 = 0$, how many iterations are needed to find the root correct to 2 decimal places? Why is the method so inefficient here?

7 Show that $x^x = \dfrac{4}{x}$ has a root in [1, 2]. Using $x_1 = 1.5$, find a better approximation by using the Newton-Raphson method once with a numerical approximation for $f'(1.5)$.

8 How many real roots has the equation $\ln x = 4 \cos x$? Find the smallest one, correct to 4 decimal places.

Numerical solutions

When an analytical solution cannot be found to a differential equation, a solution curve can be produced from a given starting point using straight line approximations. Each of the following are examples of such methods.

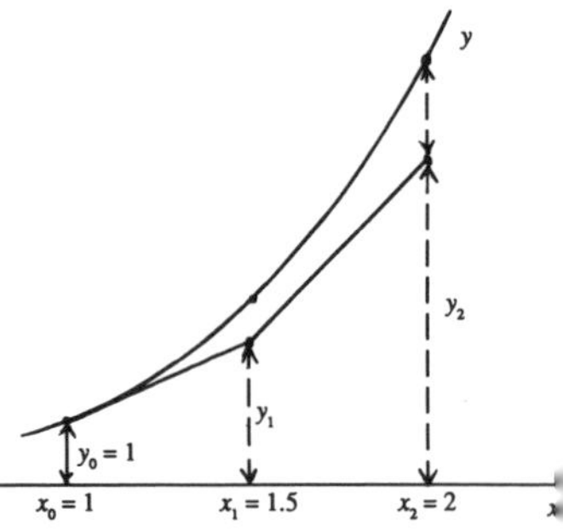

Euler's method

Differential equation:

$$\frac{dy}{dx} = g(x), \text{ starting point is } (x_0, y_0)$$

For intervals $\delta x = h$: $x_1 = x_0 + h$
$y_1 = y_0 + hg(x_0)$

This is based on the gradient calculated at the **beginning** of each interval and gives a **first order** approximation (since halving the interval halves the error).

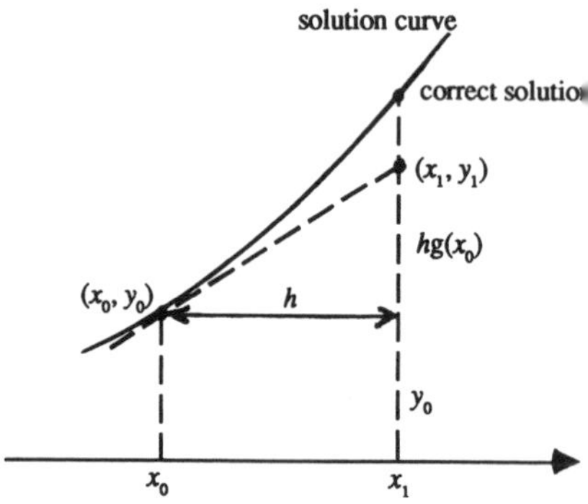

Mid-point Euler

Instead of using the gradient at the initial point of the step, use the gradient at the mid-point.

If $\frac{dy}{dx} = g(x)$ and $y = y_0$ when $x = x_0$

then $y_1 = y_0 + hg(x_0 + \frac{h}{2})$

and $x_1 = x_0 + h$

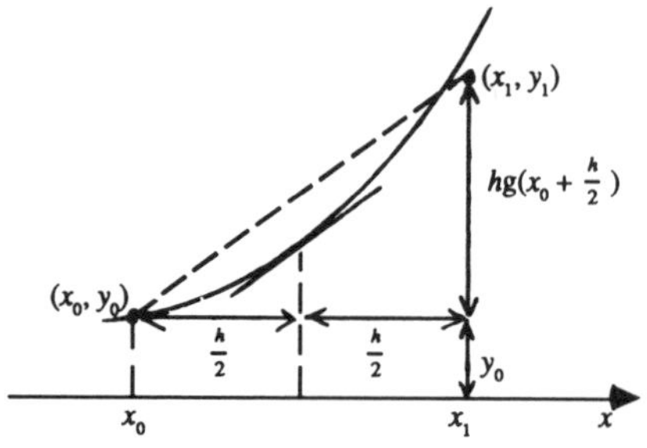

Improved Euler

Instead of using the gradient at the initial point only, use the average of the gradients at the initial point and the end point of the step.

If $\frac{dy}{dx} = g(x)$ and $y = y_0$ when $x = x_0$

then $y_1 = y_0 + h \dfrac{g(x_0) + g(x_0 + h)}{2}$

and $x_1 = x_0 + h$

Both of the above rules are **second order** approximations since halving the interval divides the error by four (2^2).

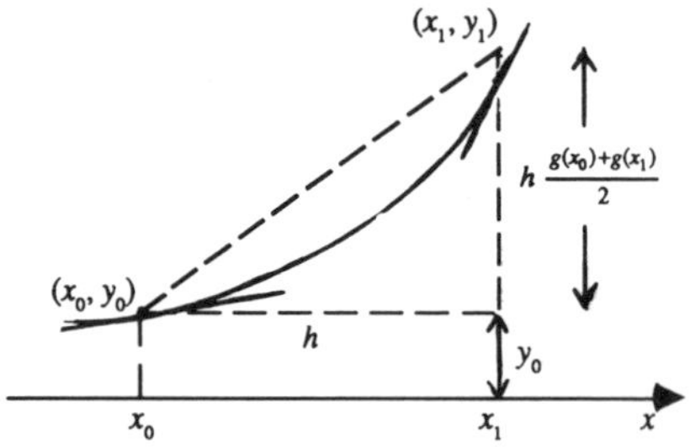

Fourth order Runge-Kutta

This calculation can be done in two ways:

(i) using $x_1 = x_0 + h$

and

$$y_1 = y_0 + h \left(\frac{g(x_0) + 4g(x_0 + \frac{h}{2}) + g(x_0 + h)}{6} \right)$$

(ii) or using the weighted average of 2:1 from the mid-point Euler and the improved Euler formulas.

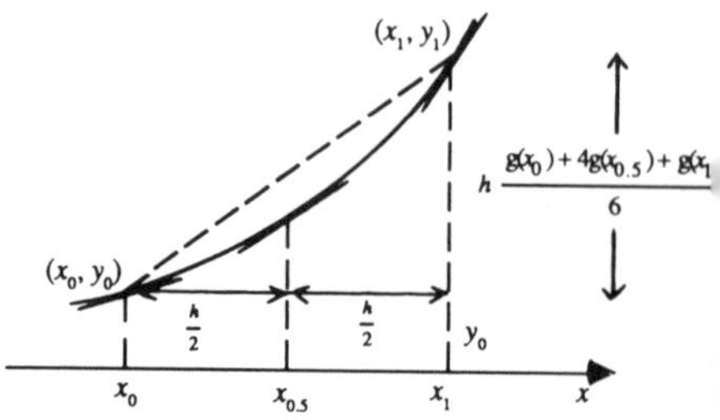

This gives a **fourth order** approximation since halving the interval divides the error by sixteen (2^4).

■ Starting from the point (0.6, 1) and using 4 steps find the solution for y at $x = 1$ when $\frac{dy}{dx} = x \sin 2x$ using:

(a) Euler's method (b) Mid-point Euler

(c) Improved Euler (d) Runge-Kutta

Confirm your result for (d) by considering the weighted average of (b) and (c) and also by direct integration.

● (a) $g(x) = x \sin 2x \quad x_0 = 0.6, h = 0.1, y_0 = 1$

$y_1 = y_0 + hg(x_0) = 1 + 0.1\ (0.6 \sin 1.2) = 1.05592$

$y_2 = y_1 + hg(x_1) = 1.05592 + 0.1\ (0.7 \sin 1.4)$

$= 1.12490$

etc. leading to (1, 1.29252) for (x_4, y_4).

(b) $y_1 = y_0 + hg(x_0 + \frac{h}{2}) = 1 + 0.1(0.65 \sin 1.3)$

$= 1.06263$

etc. leading to (1, 1.31163) for (x_4, y_4).

(c) $y_1 = y_0 + h\left(\frac{g(x_0) + g(x_0 + h)}{2}\right)$

$= 1 + 0.1\left(\frac{0.6 \sin 1.2 + 0.7 \sin 1.4}{2}\right)$

$= 1.06245$

etc. leading to (1, 1.31002) for (x_4, y_4).

(d) $y_1 = y_0 + h\left(\frac{g(x_0) + 4g(x_0 + \frac{h}{2}) + g(x_0 + h)}{6}\right)$

$= 1 + 0.1\left(\frac{0.6 \sin 1.2 + 2.6 \sin 1.3 + 0.7 \sin 1.4}{6}\right)$

$= 1.06257$

etc. leading to (1,1.31110).

Using 2 x result from (b) + result from (c) then dividing by 3 gives (1, 1.31110), confirming the result from (d).

Also $y = \int x \sin 2x\, dx$ by parts:

$u = x \qquad \frac{du}{dx} = 1$

$\frac{dv}{dx} = \sin 2x \qquad v = -\frac{1}{2}\cos 2x$

$y = -\frac{x}{2}\cos 2x + \int \frac{1}{2}\cos 2x\, dx$

$y = -\frac{x}{2}\cos 2x + \frac{1}{4}\sin 2x + c$

$x = 0.6$, when $y = 1$, so

$y = -\frac{x}{2}\cos 2x + \frac{1}{4}\sin 2x + 0.87570$

Thus at $x = 1$, $y = 1.31110$, confirming the earlier result.

1 (a) Use Euler's method and 5 steps to find a solution for $f(x)$ at $x = 3$ given that $f'(x) = e^{x^2}$ and the curve passes through the point (2, –1).

(b) Illustrate your steps on a diagram, drawing the appropriate trapezia. Would you expect your estimate to be less or more than the correct value for $f(x)$ at $x = 3$?

2 A curve has gradient $\frac{dy}{dx} = \ln|\cos x|$ and passes through the origin.

(a) Use 4 steps from the origin to find an estimate for y at $x = 0.4$ using both the mid-point Euler and the improved Euler formulas.

(b) Using the recurrence relation below find the fourth order Runge-Kutta approximation.

$$y_{n+1} = y_n + h\left(\frac{g(x_n) + 4g(x_n + \frac{h}{2}) + g(x_n + h)}{6}\right)$$

(c) Confirm that your result is the average of your answers to (a), weighted 2:1 in favour of the mid-point Euler result.

3 A gradient function of $f(x)$ is given by $g(x) = \frac{1}{1 - x^2}$, $|x| \neq 1$.

(a) Explain why you cannot start from the point (0,3) and use a step by step method to evaluate f(2).

(b) Use the improved Euler method with 4 steps from (3, 5) to evaluate the function at $x = 4$.

(c) Separate the function $g(x)$ into two partial fractions and integrate the function to find the exact value of $f(x)$ at $x = 4$.

4 Starting from the point (1, 2) and given that $f'(x) = 3x^2$, use 4 steps to find an approximate value for $f(x)$ at $x = 3$, using:

(a) Euler's method;

(b) the improved Euler formula;

(c) Runge-Kutta.

(d) Find the exact value of $f(x)$ at $x = 3$.

DIFFERENTIAL EQUATIONS

Any equation involving a derivative is called a **differential equation.**

If you differentiate a function to obtain the gradient function, you obtain a differential equation. Repeating the process gives **higher order derivatives.**

$\dfrac{d^2y}{dx^2}$ is the second derivative or the derivative of order two.

$\dfrac{d^ny}{dx^n}$ is the *n*th derivative or the derivative of order *n*.

Function notation

Function notation is often used to express higher order derivatives. Thus the first three derivatives of $f(t) = \cos 2t$ are written

$$f'(t) = -2 \sin 2t, \;\; f''(t) = -4 \cos 2t \text{ and } f^{(3)}(t) = 8 \sin 2t$$

(Note that for derivatives of order three and above, the dash notation is not often used as it is too cumbersome.)

The order of a differential equation

The order of the equation is equal to the highest order of a derivative that occurs in the equation. The following differential equations have orders 1, 3 and *m* respectively:

$$\frac{dy}{dx} = y \sin x, \;\; f^{(3)}(t) + f''(t) - f(t) = 0 \text{ and } \frac{d^m v}{dz^m} + z^2 = \frac{dv}{dz}$$

Solution by inspection

If a first order differential equation can be rearranged into the form $\dfrac{dy}{dx} = f(x)$, then it can often be solved by just integrating both sides with respect to *x*. This is known as **solution by inspection.** For higher orders, if the equation can be rearranged to obtain the form $\dfrac{d^my}{dx^m} = f(x)$, where *m* is a positive integer, the same is often true, except now it must be integrated *m* times. The result is a set of curves. If there is sufficient extra information about the solution then a **particular solution** can be found.

Numerical methods

For first order differential equations the gradient function can be used to help find numerical approximations to the exact solution. This is known as the **step-by-step method.**

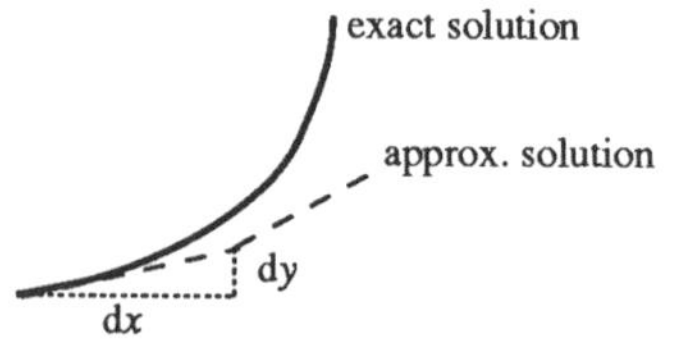

$$dy = \frac{dy}{dx}\, dx$$

For the equation $\dfrac{dy}{dx} = (1 + x)e^x$, find the approximate value of *y* when $x = 4$ for the particular solution through (3, 2) using the step method with two steps. A table provides the final summary, while detailed calculations are best done using a programmable calculator or a computer spreadsheet.

x	y	dy/dx	dx	dy	x + dx	y + dy
3	2	80.34215	0.5	40.17107	3.5	42.17107
3.5	42.17107	149.01953	0.5	74.50977	4	116.6808
4	116.6808					

The accuracy of this method is affected by the step size. The smaller the step, the more accurate the approximation. Consider the effect on the example above. A step size of 0.1 will give $y = 150.7$, much closer to the actual value of 160.1.

■ A particle moves such that at time t seconds, the displacement from a fixed point (in metres) is given by the equation $f(t) = t^3 - 6t^2 + 9t$. Find the velocity and acceleration after 2 seconds and show that the particle is at rest on just two occasions.

● $f'(t) = 3t^2 - 12t + 9 \Rightarrow v = -3 \text{ ms}^{-1}$ when $t = 2$ seconds

$f''(t) = 6t - 12 \Rightarrow a = 0 \text{ ms}^{-2}$ when $t = 2$ seconds

$v = 0$ when $3t^2 - 12t + 9 = 0$, which has exactly 2 solutions when $t = 1$ and $t = 3$.

■ Find the general solution for each of the following.

(a) $\frac{d^2z}{dx^2} = 6 \sin 3x$ (b) $x^3 \frac{d^2y}{dx^2} + 1 = x$

● (a) $\frac{d^2z}{dx^2} = 6 \sin 3x$

$\frac{dz}{dx} = -2 \cos 3x + k$

$\Rightarrow z = -\frac{2}{3} \sin 3x + kx + c$

(b) $x^3 \frac{d^2y}{dx^2} + 1 = x$

$\frac{d^2y}{dx^2} = \frac{1}{x^2} - \frac{1}{x^3}$

$\Rightarrow \frac{dy}{dx} = \frac{-1}{x} + \frac{1}{2x^2} + k$

$\Rightarrow y = -\ln x - \frac{1}{2x} + kx + c$

■ If $y'' = 6(x + 2x^2)$, find the solution curve that passes through (0, 4) and (1, 7).

● $y'' = 6(x + 2x^2) \Rightarrow y' = 3x^2 + 4x^3 + k$

$\Rightarrow y = x^3 + x^4 + kx + c$

$(0, 4) \Rightarrow c = 4$, and (1, 7) then gives $k = 1$. So the solution is $y = x^3 + x^4 + x + 4$.

■ $\frac{dF}{dT} = \frac{100 - F}{5 + F}$

Using four intervals, find a numerical approximation for F when $T = 2$, given that when $T = 0$, $F = 10$. Comment on the behaviour of F as T increases.

●

T	F	dF/dT	dT	dF
0	10	6	0.5	3
0.5	13	4.83	0.5	2.42
1	15.42	4.14	0.5	2.07
1.5	17.49	3.67	0.5	1.83
2	19.32			

So when $T = 2$, an approximation for F is 19.32. As time increases, the rate of change of F decreases, but without an analytic solution you still cannot tell if the value of F is bounded.

1 (a) (i) Find the third derivative of $y = e^{5x}$.

(ii) What is the nth derivative?

(b) What is the nth derivative of $y = \ln x$?

2 If $y = \cos \omega x$ find $\frac{d^2y}{dx^2}$ in terms of y and ω.

3 (a) Find the general solution for each of the following differential equations:

(i) $\frac{d^3z}{dx^3} = 18 \sin 2x - x^4$

(ii) $x^3 \frac{d^2y}{dx^2} + 5x^4 - 2 = 0$

(iii) $\frac{dy}{dx} - 3 \sin^2 x \cos x = 0$

(b) For (ii) above, find the particular solution that passes through the points (1, 3) and (2, 5).

4 A particle moves along the x-axis, in such a way that its position at time t is given by:

$$x = 27 - 36t + 12t^2 - t^3$$

(a) Find the two times when the particle changes direction.

(b) Find the accelerations at the instants when the particle is at rest.

5 Find solutions of

$$\frac{dy}{dx} = \frac{10x}{y + 3} \text{ for } -1 \le x \le 3$$

using a step size of 0.5, with the initial values:

(a) (–1, –10)

(b) (–1, 0)

(c) (–1, –5)

Numerical solutions

The numerical step-by-step method of obtaining an approximate solution to a differential equation can be extended.

Parametric equations

Differential equations in which x and y and their derivatives are expressed in terms of a parameter t are called parametric equations.

For example, $\frac{dx}{dt} = f(x, y, t)$ and $\frac{dy}{dt} = g(x, y, t)$.

Solution curves can be plotted in the (t, x) plane and/or (t, y) plane and/or (x, y) plane.

Simultaneous linear equations

If two (or more) differential equations are used to describe a single situation, then they must be solved together at the same time (simultaneously).

A time-step, dt, needs to be chosen, or specified. The differential equations are used to estimate the steps dx, dy by following the tangent in the (t, x) and (t, y) planes. The estimated new coordinates are $(t + dt, x + dx, y + dy)$. The process is repeated starting from this point.

■ Find x and y after 2 minutes if $\frac{dx}{dt} = -0.3x + 0.5y$, $\frac{dy}{dt} = 0.3x - 0.5y$ and $x = 3$, $y = 1$ at $t = 0$.

● Let the time-step be $dt = 0.5$. $dx = (-0.3x + 0.5y)dt$, $dy = (0.3x - 0.5y)dt$.

t	x	y	dt	dx	dy
0	3	1	0.5	−0.2	0.2
0.5	2.8	1.2	0.5	−0.12	0.12
1	2.68	1.32	0.5	−0.07	0.07
1.5	2.61	1.39	0.5	−0.04	0.04
2	2.57	1.43			

The differential equations describe a chemical reaction in which no matter is lost, so $x + y = 4$ and $dx = -dy$ at all times.

Note also $\frac{d}{dt}(x + y) = \frac{dx}{dt} + \frac{dy}{dt} = 0$.

Second order linear equations

A differential equation is of the second order if it contains a second derivative, e.g. $\frac{d^2x}{dt^2}$, $\frac{d^2q}{dt^2}$. A second order equation can be written as two simultaneous first order equations by introducing another variable.

■ Obtain a numerical solution to $\frac{d^2x}{dt^2} - 5\frac{dx}{dt} - 14x = 0$ if $\frac{dx}{dt} = 2$ and $x = 0$ at $t = 0$:

(i) in $0 \le t \le 2$ using a step of $dt = 0.5$; (ii) in $0 \le t \le 0.5$ using a step of $dt = 0.1$.

● Let $V = \frac{dx}{dt}$, so that $\frac{dV}{dt} = \frac{d^2x}{dt^2}$. The numerical solution is built up using $dx = V dt$ and $dV = (5V + 14x)\,dt$.

	t	x	V	dt	dx	dV
	0	0	2	0.5	1	5
	0.5	1	7	0.5	3.5	24.5
	1	4.5	31.5	0.5	15.75	110.25
	1.5	20.25	141.8	0.5	70.9	496
	2	91	638			
	0	0	2	0.1	0.2	1
	0.1	0.2	3	0.1	0.3	1.78
	⋮	⋮	⋮	⋮	⋮	⋮
	0.4	1.77	13.17	0.1	1.32	9.06
	0.5	3	22			
exact	0.5	7.3	51.7			

When $dt = 0.5$, the large values obtained for dx and dV suggest the numerical solution is very inaccurate. The exact solution is

$$x = \frac{1}{9}(2e^{7t} - 2e^{-2t})$$

$$V = \frac{dx}{dt} = \frac{1}{9}(14e^{7t} + 4e^{-2t})$$

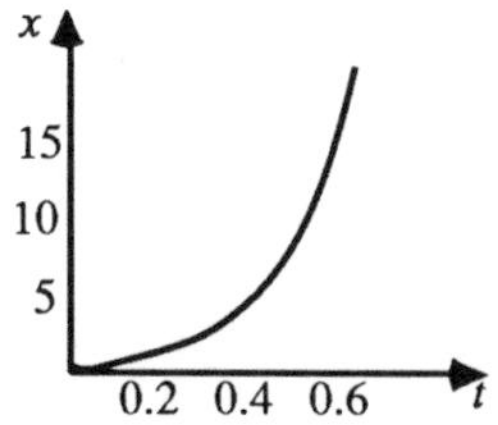

The inaccuracy is due to the dominance of e^{7t} in the exact solution ($t > 0$). The gradient increases very rapidly for small increments in t.

■ Estimate the current flowing in the circuit for $0 \le t \le 1$ if $i = q = 0$ at $t = 0$.

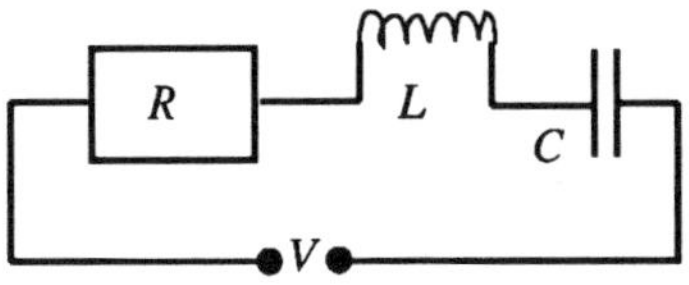

resistance: R ohms
inductance: L henries
capacitance: C farads
voltage: V volts

The current i amps, and charge q coulombs satisfy:

$$\frac{di}{dt} + \frac{R}{L}i + \frac{q}{LC} = \frac{V}{L}; \quad i = \frac{dq}{dt}$$

● Let $V = 8, L = 4, R = 10, C = 5, dt = 0.2, dq = i\,dt$, $di = (2 - 2.5i - 0.05q)\,dt$.

t	i	q	dt	di	dq
0	0	0	0.2	0.4	0
0.2	0.4	0	0.2	0.2	0.08
0.4	0.6	0.08	0.2	0.099	0.12
0.6	0.699	0.2	0.2	0.049	0.14
0.8	0.748	0.34	0.2	0.023	0.15
1	0.77	0.49			

■ A parachutist falls from rest for 5 seconds. Use the differential equation

$$m\frac{dV}{dt} + kV - mg = 0$$

to estimate the displacement and velocity in this interval if $\frac{k}{m} = 0.2$, $g = 10$ and $dt = 1$.

● $dx = V dt$ $\qquad dV = (10 - 0.2V)\,dt$

t	V	x	dt	dV	dx
0	0	0	1	10	0
1	10	0	1	8	10
2	18	10	1	6.4	18
3	24.4	28	1	5.1	24.4
4	29.5	52.4	1	4.1	29.5
5	33.6	81.9			

In fact, V is tending to a constant value of 50 ms^{-1}, the terminal velocity of the parachutist.

1 A stunt girl leaps from a bridge attached to an elastic rope. Her distance x metres below the bridge is given by

$$\frac{dx}{dt} = u + 5, \quad \frac{du}{dt} = -2x - 2u$$

where t is the time, in seconds, after the elastic rope becomes taut. At $t = 0$, $x = 20$ and $u = 15$.

(a) Using a time-step of $dt = 0.5$, estimate the girl's speed 1 second after the rope becomes taut.

(b) Find the second order differential equation with variables x and t only for which this is an approximate solution.

2 The differential equation $\frac{dV}{dt} = 10 - 0.1V^2$ is generally accepted as a better model for a falling parachutist than that in the example above.

(a) Attempt a numerical solution with time-step $dt = 1$, if the parachutist is descending at 15 ms^{-1} when she opens her parachute. What problem is encountered?

(b) Show that the exact solution is

$$V = 10\,\frac{(5 + e^{-2t})}{(5 - e^{-2t})}$$

and use this to explain why the above problem occurs. Suggest a time-step that will show the long-term behaviour of the parachutist.

3 The suspension system of a beach buggy has a spring with a shock absorber to damp the vibrations. The vertical height y of the chassis, t seconds after a wheel hits a bump, is given by:

$$500\frac{d^2y}{dt^2} = -120y - 40\frac{dy}{dt}$$

Show that this can be represented by the two simultaneous first order differential equations

$$\frac{dy}{dt} = V \text{ and } \frac{dV}{dt} = -0.08V - 0.24y$$

If $y = 0$ and $\frac{dy}{dt} = 10$ when $t = 0$, sketch a graph of y against t for $0 \le t \le 16$, using $dt = 2$.

4 A radioactive substance P decays and changes without loss of mass into a substance Q, which in turn changes to a third substance R.

The masses of P, Q and R at time t are given by p, q and r grams. The rates of change are such that

$$\frac{dp}{dt} = -2p \quad \frac{dr}{dt} = q, \text{ and } p = 1, q = 0, r = 0 \text{ at } t = 0.$$

(a) Show that $\frac{dq}{dt} = 2p - q$.

(b) Use numerical integration with $dt = 0.2$ to estimate p, q and r after 1 second. Use graphs to illustrate what happens as time continues.

Separable variables

A differential equation of the form $g(y)\frac{dy}{dx} = f(x)$ will yield a solution by separating the variables i.e.

$$\int g(y)dy = \int f(x)dx$$

This method will work for equations such as

$$\frac{dy}{dx} = y(x^2 + 1) \qquad \text{or } (x^2 + 1)\frac{dy}{dx} = xy$$

but not

$$\frac{dy}{dx} = yx^2 + 1 \qquad \text{or } \frac{dy}{dx} = x + y$$

Particular integral

A particular integral (PI) for an equation which cannot be solved by separating variables can often be found by trying a suitable function.

■ Find the PI of $\frac{dy}{dx} + 0.05y = 0.2 - 0.01x$.

● Try $y = Ax + B \Rightarrow \frac{dy}{dx} = A$

$\Rightarrow A + 0.05\,(Ax + B) = 0.2 - 0.01x$ [sub in differential equation]

Compare coefficients of x: $0.05A = -0.01 \Rightarrow A = -0.2$

Compare constants: $A + 0.05B = 0.2 \Rightarrow B = 8$

PI is $y = 8 - 0.2x$.

The type of function tried will reflect the nature of the right-hand side of the equation. For example:

$\frac{dy}{dx} + 0.6y = 1.6x^2$ try $y = Ax^2 + Bx + C$

$\frac{dy}{dx} + 0.6y = 1.6 \sin 2x$ try $y = A \sin 2x + B \cos 2x$

Linear equations

A first order linear differential equation has the form

$$\frac{dy}{dx} + p(x)y = q(x)$$

The complementary function (CF) is the solution of the equation

$$\frac{dy}{dx} + p(x)y = 0.$$

By using the additive property of solutions of a linear differential equation, the general solution can be expressed as the sum of the complementary function (CF) and the particular integral (PI).

■ (a) Solve the differential equation $\frac{dy}{dx} = \frac{2x}{3y^2}$

(b) Find the equation of the particular solution which passes through (1, 2).

● (a) $3y^2 dy = 2x dx$

$\Rightarrow \int 3y^2 dy = \int 2x dx$

$\Rightarrow \quad y^3 = x^2 + c$

(b) Using (1, 2) $\Rightarrow 8 = 1 + c$

$\Rightarrow c = 7$

Particular solution is $y^3 = x^2 + 7$.

■ (a) Solve the differential equation $\frac{dy}{dx} + y = 0$.

(b) Solve the differential equation $\frac{dy}{dx} + y = 2e^{3x}$ given that $y = 2$ when $x = 0$.

● (a) $\frac{dy}{dx} = -y \Rightarrow \frac{1}{y}\,dy = -dx \Rightarrow \int \frac{1}{y}\,dy = \int -dx$

$\Rightarrow \ln y = -x + c$

$\Rightarrow \quad y = Ae^{-x}$

(b) **PI** Try $y = Ke^{3x} \Rightarrow \frac{dy}{dx} = 3Ke^{3x}$

$\Rightarrow 3Ke^{3x} + Ke^{3x} = 2e^{3x}$

$\Rightarrow K = \frac{1}{2}$

$\Rightarrow y = \frac{1}{2}e^{3x}$ is a particular integral.

CF Solve $\frac{dy}{dx} + y = 0 \Rightarrow y = Ae^{-x}$

General solution is $y = Ae^{-x} + \frac{1}{2}e^{3x}$.

Using (0, 2) $\Rightarrow 2 = A + \frac{1}{2} \Rightarrow A = \frac{3}{2}$

Particular solution is $y = \frac{3}{2}e^{-x} + \frac{1}{2}e^{3x}$.

■ Solve the differential equation

$$\frac{dh}{dt} - 4h = 2\sin 3t$$

given that $h = 1$ when $t = 0$.

● Let $\frac{dh}{dt} - 4h = 0$

$\Rightarrow \int \frac{1}{h}\,dh = \int 4dt$

$\Rightarrow \ln h = 4t + c \qquad$ i.e. $h = Ke^{4t} \qquad$ (CF)

Now try $h = A\sin 3t + B\cos 3t$

$\Rightarrow \frac{dh}{dt} = 3A\cos 3t - 3B\sin 3t$

So $(3A\cos 3t - 3B\sin 3t) - 4(A\sin 3t + B\cos 3t)$
$= 2\sin 3t$

Compare coefficients of $\cos 3t$: $3A - 4B = 0$
$\sin 3t$: $-3B - 4A = 2$

So $B = -0.24$ and $A = -0.32$

General solution is $h = Ke^{4t} - 0.32\sin 3t - 0.24\cos 3t$

Using $h = 1, t = 0 \Rightarrow 1 = K - 0.24$
i.e. $K = 1.24$

Particular solution is

$$y = 1.24e^{4t} - 0.32\sin 3t - 0.24\cos 3t$$

1 Solve the differential equations:

(a) $\frac{dy}{dx} = 3y^2$ (b) $x\frac{dy}{dx} - y + 4 = 0$

2 Solve the differential equation $(x^2 + 1)\frac{dy}{dx} = x$ given that $y = 0$ when $x = 1$.

3 Solve the differential equation $\frac{dv}{dt} = 4 - v^2$ given that $v = 0$ when $t = 0$.

4 Find a particular integral for each of the following differential equations.

(a) $\frac{dv}{dt} - 2v = t^2 - 1$

(b) $\frac{dy}{dt} + y = 0.5\sin 2t$

(c) $\frac{dy}{dt} - 3y = e^{3t}$

5 Find general solutions for the differential equations:

(a) $\frac{dy}{dx} + \frac{1}{2}y = 6$ (b) $\frac{dv}{dx} - 3v = 2e^x$

6 Solve the differential equation:

$\frac{dy}{dx} + 4y = 2x - 1$ given $y = \frac{1}{2}$ when $x = 0$

7 Find the particular solution of the following equation, given that $y = 0$ when $x = \frac{\pi}{6}$.

$$\frac{dy}{dx} = \sqrt{(1 - y^2)}$$

8 Solve the differential equation

$$(1 + \cos 2\theta)\frac{dy}{d\theta} = 2$$

if $y = 1$ when $\theta = \frac{\pi}{4}$.

Arbitrary constants

The general solution of a differential equation of order *n* has *n* **arbitrary constants.** If the solution satisfies *n* initial conditions (or boundary conditions), then the values of the constants can be determined, giving rise to a particular solution.

Linearity

The general solution of the equation

$$a\frac{d^2y}{dx^2} + b\frac{dy}{dx} + cy = f(x)$$

is the sum of a **particular integral** and the **complementary function** (with two arbitrary constants).

If a particular solution is required, use two boundary conditions to determine the value of the two arbitrary constants.

The complementary function

For the differential equation

$$a\frac{d^2y}{dx^2} + b\frac{dy}{dx} + cy = f(x)$$

the equation $am^2 + bm + c = 0$ is called the **auxiliary equation.**

If the roots of the auxiliary equation are α and β, then the **complementary function** is $Ae^{\alpha x} + Be^{\beta x}$.

The particular integral

To find a particular integral it is usual to assume that it has the same form as f(x) and then use the differential equation to determine values for any constants. A particular integral must be distinct from the complementary function so if f(x) has the same form as part of the complementary function an alternative particular integral must be sought.

For example,

$$\frac{d^2y}{dx^2} - \frac{4dy}{dx} + 3y = e^x$$

has CF $y = Ae^{3x} + Be^x$ and so a PI of $y = Ce^x$ is already included in the CF. An alternative PI of $y = Cxe^x$ should be used.

Repeated roots

If an auxiliary equation has a repeated root α, then the complementary function is $y = (Ax + B)e^{\alpha x}$.

Complex roots

If the roots of the auxiliary equation are $v \pm \omega j$ then the complementary function is of the form $y = e^{vx}(A \cos \omega x + B \sin \omega x)$.

Substitution

The following types of differential equations can be solved by symbolic methods:

- first order equations with separable variables;
- first order linear equations;
- second order linear equations with constant coefficients.

Sometimes other differential equations can be transformed into one of these equations by means of a suitable substitution.

To transform a differential equation:

- find all the derivatives in terms of the new variables;
- substitute for these derivatives in the original equation.

■ Find the general solution of

$$\frac{d^2x}{dt^2} - 2\frac{dx}{dt} - 3x = 5\sin 3t.$$

● Auxiliary equation $m^2 - 2m - 3 = 0$
$\Rightarrow (m+1)(m-3) = 0$
$\Rightarrow m = -1$ or $m = 3$

Therefore CF is $x = Ae^{-t} + Be^{3t}$.

For a PI try $x = P\sin 3t + Q\cos 3t$

$$\Rightarrow \frac{dx}{dt} = 3P\cos 3t - 3Q\sin 3t$$

and $$\frac{d^2x}{dt^2} = -9P\sin 3t - 9Q\cos 3t$$

Substituting into the original equation gives:
$(-9P\sin 3t - 9Q\cos 3t) - 2(3P\cos 3t - 3Q\sin 3t) - 3(P\sin 3t + Q\cos 3t) = 5\sin 3t$
$\Rightarrow (-12P + 6Q)\sin 3t - (6P + 12Q)\cos 3t = 5\sin 3t$

equating coefficients

$\Rightarrow -12P + 6Q = 5$ and $6P + 12Q = 0$

$\Rightarrow P = -\frac{1}{3}$ and $Q = \frac{1}{6}$

The PI is $x = \frac{1}{6}\cos 3t - \frac{1}{3}\sin 3t$ and the general solution is $x = Ae^{-t} + Be^{3t} + \frac{1}{6}\cos 3t - \frac{1}{3}\sin 3t$.

■ By means of the substitution $y = zx$ where z is a function of x, solve the equation

$$x\frac{dy}{dx} - y = x^2 + y^2$$

given that $y = 0$ when $x = \frac{\pi}{2}$.

● $y = zx \Rightarrow \frac{dy}{dx} = z + x\frac{dz}{dx}$ and substituting into the original equation gives:

$$x\left(z + x\frac{dz}{dx}\right) - zx = x^2 + (zx)^2 \Rightarrow x^2\frac{dz}{dx} = x^2 + z^2x^2$$

$$\Rightarrow \frac{dz}{dx} = 1 + z^2$$

Hence $\int \frac{dz}{1+z^2} = \int dx \Rightarrow \tan^{-1}z = x + c$

$$\Rightarrow \tan^{-1}\frac{y}{x} = x + c$$

Given that $y = 0$ when $x = \frac{\pi}{2}$, $\tan^{-1}(0) = \frac{\pi}{2} + c$

$$\Rightarrow c = -\frac{\pi}{2}$$

$$\tan^{-1}\frac{y}{x} = x - \frac{\pi}{2} \Rightarrow \frac{y}{x} = \tan\left(x - \frac{\pi}{2}\right)$$

$$\Rightarrow y = x\tan\left(x - \frac{\pi}{2}\right)$$

1 Find the general solution of the following equations:

(a) $\frac{d^2y}{dx^2} + 6\frac{dy}{dx} + 9y = 0$

(b) $\frac{d^2y}{dx^2} - 3\frac{dy}{dx} + 3y = 0$

(c) $\frac{d^2x}{dt^2} - \frac{dx}{dt} - 2x = 8\sin 2t$

(d) $\frac{d^2y}{dx^2} - \frac{dy}{dx} - 6y = 5e^{-2x}$

(e) $\frac{d^2y}{dx^2} + 2\frac{dy}{dx} + y = x^2 - 3$

2 Solve the differential equation

$$\frac{d^2y}{dx^2} - 4\frac{dy}{dx} + 3y = e^{3x}$$

given that $y = 1$ and $\frac{dy}{dx} = 0$ when $x = 0$.

3 If $x = 0$ and $\frac{dx}{dt} = 7$ when $t = 0$, solve the differential equation:

$$2\frac{d^2x}{dt^2} - 5\frac{dx}{dt} - 3x = 0$$

4 Find the general solution of the differential equation

$$\frac{d^2y}{dx^2} - 4\frac{dy}{dx} + 4y = 13\cos 3x$$

Find also the particular solution for which $y = 1$ and $\frac{dy}{dx} = 0$ when $x = 0$.

5 Use the substitution $y = z + x^2$ to help solve the equation:

$$\frac{d^2y}{dx^2} - x^2 + y - 2 = 0$$

6 (a) An object oscillates such that its displacement x from its equilibrium position is modelled by the equation:

$$\frac{d^2x}{dt^2} + 4x = 0$$

Solve this differential equation, given that $x = 3$ and $\frac{dx}{dt} = 0$ when $t = 0$.

(b) A frictional force and a periodic disturbing force are introduced into the system and the new equation of motion is:

$$\frac{d^2x}{dt^2} + 5\frac{dx}{dt} + 4x = 4\sin t + \cos t$$

Solve this equation subject to the same initial conditions.

MISCELLANEOUS EXERCISES

MATHEMATICAL STRUCTURE

1 Construct and compare combination tables for:

(a) $\{0, 1, 2\}$ under addition modulo 3;

(b) $\{1, 2, 3\}$ under multiplication modulo 4;

(c) the group of rotations of an equilateral triangle.

2 A binary operation, *, on the set of real numbers is defined by

$$a * b = a + b - ab$$

Show that 0 is the identity and check whether * is commutative and/or associative.

3 (a) Compile combination tables for:

$G = \{2, 4, 6, 8\}$
under multiplication modulo 10

$H = \{1, -1, j, -j\}$
under multiplication, where $j^2 = -1$

(b) Prove that G and H are ismorphic.

4 Use the laws of Boolean algebra to simplify:

(a) $(a \cap b) \cup (a \cap b') \cup (a' \cap b)$

(b) $[(a \cap b) \cup a']'$

5 (a) Write down the Boolean expression equivalent to the switching circuit drawn below.

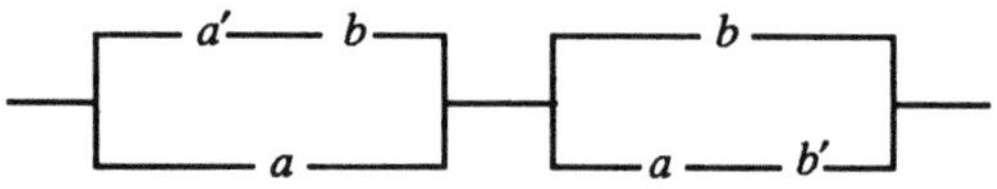

(b) Simplify this expression and hence draw an equivalent simplified version of the circuit.

6 (a) For each element of the group $\{1, 2, 3, 4\}$ under multiplication modulo 5, find the cyclic subgroup it generates.

(b) Is the group itself cyclic? Justify your answer.

7 R and T are functions such that

$$\mathrm{R}(x) = -x,\ x \in \mathbb{R}$$
$$\mathrm{T}(x) = x + 1,\ x \in \mathbb{R}$$

(a) Prove that RT is a self-inverse function.

(b) Find a function generated by R and T which maps x to $x - 10$.

8 The group R of rotations of a regular tetrahedron has 12 elements.

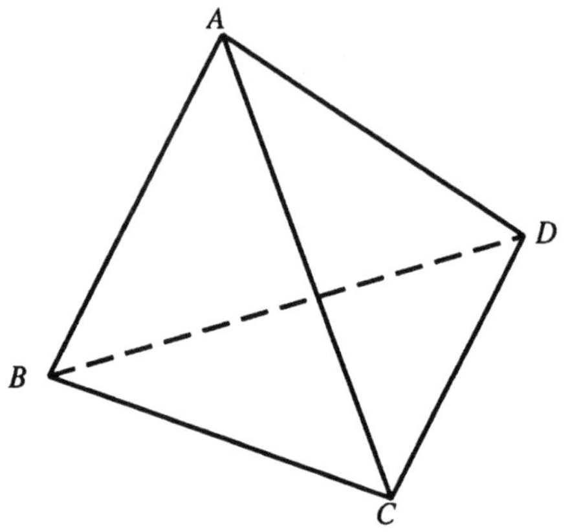

(a) By describing each possible rotation, show that R has:

one element of order 1;

three elements of order 2;

eight elements of order 3.

(b) Show that the elements of order 1 and 2 form a subgroup isomorphic to K.

(c) Explain why R has precisely one subgroup of order 4.

9 Show that

$$2 \times 1! + 5 \times 2! + 10 \times 3! + \ldots + (n^2 + 1) \times n! = n(n + 1)!$$

for all positive integers n.

10 Show, by induction or otherwise, that for all positive integers n, $5^n - 2^n$ is divisible by 3.

11 Prove, by induction or otherwise, that

$$\sum_{r=1}^{n} \frac{1}{r(r+2)} = \frac{n(3n+5)}{4(n+1)(n+2)}$$

MATRICES

1 A matrix transformation **M** maps the points P(1, 0) to itself, Q(0, 1) to Q′(2, 1) and R(1, 1) to R′(3, 1).

(a) Write down the matrix which represents the transformation **M**.

(b) Describe the matrix **M** geometrically.

(c) Find the matrix $\mathbf{M}^{-1}$ and describe the geometrical transformation it represents.

2 When a very strange coin is tossed repeatedly, the result of one toss has an effect on the next toss such that

P(head following head) = 0.4
P(tail following tail) = 0.4

(a) Write down a transition matrix to describe these probabilities.

(b) Given that the first of a series of tosses is a head, find the probability that the third toss in the series is also a head.

(c) One of the eigenvalues for the matrix obtained in (a) is 1. Find a corresponding eigenvector.

(d) Hence or otherwise, write down the long term probability that a particular toss is a head.

3 The point A is transformed by the matrix

$$\begin{bmatrix} -2 & 3 \\ 1 & 5 \end{bmatrix}$$

to the point (0, 13). What are the coordinates of A?

4 Solve the equations:

$$2x - 3y + z = 1$$
$$3x + 5y - 4z = 30$$
$$4x - y + 2z = 17$$

5 Let **R** be the matrix of reflection in the line $y = 3x$.

(a) State two eigenvectors of **R** and the corresponding eigenvalues.

(b) Write down a matrix **U** and a diagonal matrix **D** such that $\mathbf{R} = \mathbf{UDU}^{-1}$. Hence show that

$$\mathbf{R} = \frac{1}{5}\begin{bmatrix} -4 & 3 \\ 3 & 4 \end{bmatrix}$$

6 Show that the equations

$$4x - 2y + 3z = 1$$
$$3x + y - z = 7$$
$$x + 17y - 22z = 44$$

form a sheaf.

7 Let $\mathbf{T} = \begin{bmatrix} p & 0 \\ q & 1 \end{bmatrix} \quad (p \neq 1)$

(a) Show that $\begin{bmatrix} 0 \\ 1 \end{bmatrix}$ and $\begin{bmatrix} p-1 \\ q \end{bmatrix}$ are eigenvectors of **T** and find the correponding eigenvalues.

(b) Given that $p = q = \frac{1}{2}$, find a matrix **U** and a diagonal matrix **D** such that

$$\mathbf{T} = \mathbf{UDU}^{-1}$$

Hence, or otherwise, show that

$$\mathbf{T}^n = \begin{bmatrix} \left(\frac{1}{2}\right)^n & 0 \\ 1 - \left(\frac{1}{2}\right)^n & 1 \end{bmatrix} \quad (n \geq 1)$$

8 Use Gaussian elimination with partial pivoting to solve the equations

$$2.0x_1 + 1.0x_2 + 1.0x_3 = 3.4$$
$$1.0x_1 + 4.5x_2 + 3.5x_3 = 1.7$$
$$1.0x_1 - 1.5x_2 + 5.5x_3 = 22.5$$

9 Use the LU decomposition method to solve the equations

$$\begin{bmatrix} 2 & 1 & 1 \\ 3 & 4 & 1 \\ 1 & 1 & 2 \end{bmatrix}\begin{bmatrix} x_1 \\ x_2 \\ x_3 \end{bmatrix} = \begin{bmatrix} 6 \\ 17 \\ 3 \end{bmatrix}$$

10 For the simultaneous equations:

$$x + 2y - 2z = -2$$
$$3x + 4y - 2z = d$$
$$x + 4y + cz = -7$$

(a) Find a canonical form.

(b) When $c = -5$ and $d = 4$, obtain the solution.

(c) When $c = -6$,

(i) state the value of d which gives infinitely many solutions;

(ii) write down the solution in this case.

COMPLEX NUMBERS

1 Solve:

(a) $z^3 + 8 = 0$

(b) $z^3 - 11z^2 + 36z - 26 = 0$

2 If $z_1 = 1 + j$ and $z_2 = 3 - 4j$, find $\left|\dfrac{z_1}{z_2}\right|$ and $\arg\left(\dfrac{z_1}{z_2}\right)$.

3 Find $(1 - j)^{16}$.

4 $P(r, \theta)$ is a point on the circle given by

$$|z - 4j| = 4$$

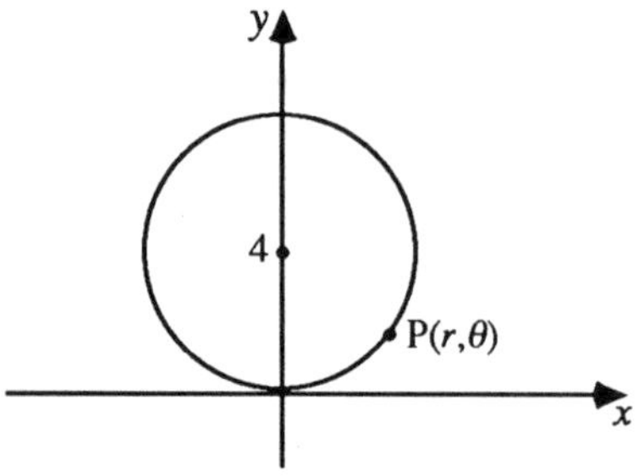

(a) Show that $r = 8 \sin \theta$.

(b) If $P'[R, \phi]$ is the image of P under the transformation $z \to z^2$, show that $R = 32(1 - \cos \phi)$.

(c) Sketch the graph of the image set.

5 (a) Describe the locus of z such that

$$|z - 1| = 3|z - 5|$$

(b) What is the image of this locus under the mapping $z \to (\sqrt{3} + j)z$?

6 Given that Re(z) denotes the real part of z and Im(z) denotes the imaginary part, sketch the image of

$$\{z : x \geq y, 0 \leq x \leq 2, 0 \leq y \leq 2\}$$

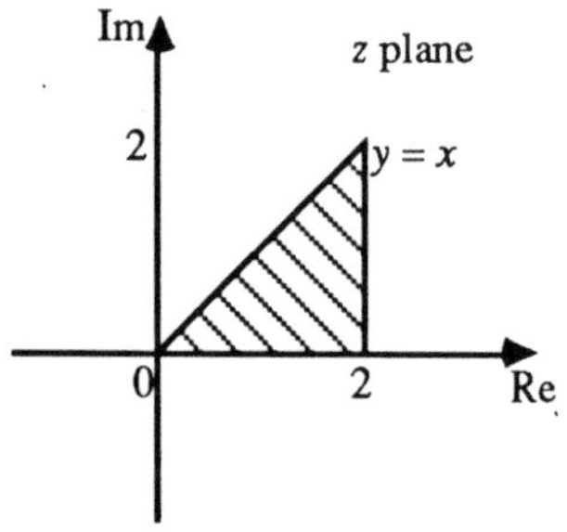

under the mapping $z \to \dfrac{jz}{2} - j$.

7 Use the definition of cos z to prove that

$$2\cos^2 z - 1 = \cos 2z$$

8 Find the image of 8 and $6j$ under the transformation $z \to \dfrac{1}{z}$ and hence sketch the image of $|z - 4 - 3j| = 5$ under this transformation.

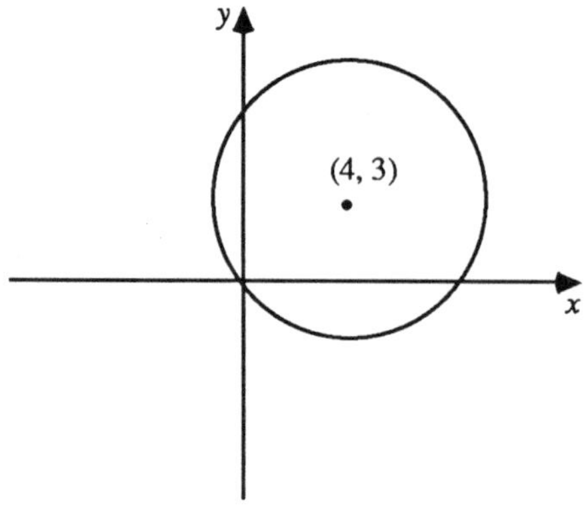

9 Express $\dfrac{3z - 1}{z + 3}$ in the form $\alpha + \dfrac{\beta}{z + \gamma}$ and hence describe the transformation $z \to \dfrac{3z - 1}{z + 3}$ as a combination of transformations.

10 Find the fixed points in the system defined by

$$z_{n+1} = z_n^2 + 1$$

11 Find the value of a such that

$$z_{n+1} = j - az_n, \; z_0 = j$$

is periodic with period 2.

12 (a) Express $\dfrac{jz}{z + 1}$ in the form $\alpha + \dfrac{\beta}{z + \gamma}$.

(b) Hence, or otherwise, find the image of

$$|z + 3| = 1$$

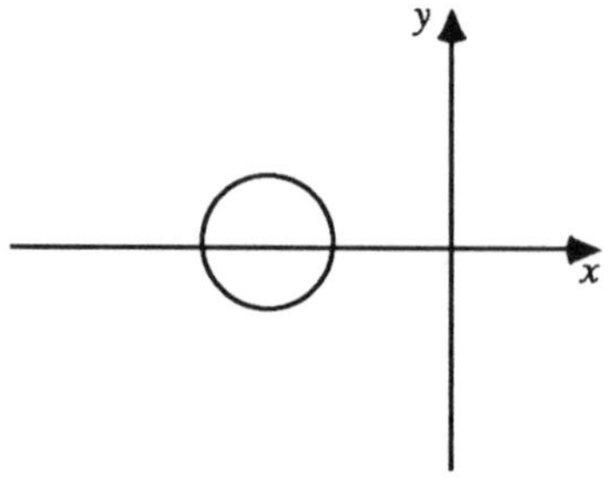

under the transformation:

$$z \to \frac{jz}{z + 1}$$

NUMERICAL METHODS

1 A manufacturer requires cubical tanks such that the volume of each tank is accurate to within 6%.

What is the maximum percentage error which is allowable in the length of each side?

2 James was asked to find an area by integration. The answer should have been 16 square units, but, instead of integrating algebraically, James used a numerical method.

With 8 strips he obtained the answer 16.0625 and with 16 strips he obtained the answer 16.015625.

(a) What was the order of accuracy of his method?

(b) Name two numerical methods he might have been using.

3 Use Simpson's rule with 4 strips to find an estimate for

$$\int_1^2 \log_{10} x \, dx$$

4 The mean value of a function $f(x)$ from $x = a$ to $x = b$ is defined as

$$\frac{1}{b-a} \int_a^b f(x) \, dx$$

Use Simpson's rule with 6 strips to find the mean value of $\sqrt{\sin x}$ from 0 to $\frac{\pi}{2}$.

5 Show that Taylor's second approximation to

$$g(x) = \frac{1}{(1+2x)}$$

at $x = 1$ is given by:

$$\frac{1}{27}(19 - 14x + 4x^2)$$

6 Show that Taylor's second approximation to $C(x) = \cos x$, centred at $x = 0$, is

$$c(x) = 1 - \frac{1}{2}x^2$$

By considering the absolute values of the error, examine how good this approximation $c(x)$ is for $-2 \le x \le 2$.

Demonstrate by sketching $c(x)$ and $C(x)$ on the same axes for a suitable range of values of x.

7 Find the Taylor series for

$$\frac{4}{(5+x)}$$

centred on $x = 0$.

State the radius of convergence of this series.

By using $x = \frac{1}{5}$, use your series to find $\frac{4}{13}$ correct to 5 decimal places. Explain why $x = 8$ cannot be used to find the value of $\frac{4}{13}$.

8 (a) Show that the equation

$$x^3 - 4x - 2 = 0$$

has roots in the intervals [–2, –1], [–1, 0] and [2, 3].

(b) Show how the equation leads to the iterative formula:

$$x_{n+1} = \frac{x_n^3}{4} - 0.5$$

By means of a sketch show that the sequence will only ever converge to the middle root. Find this root correct to 2 decimal places.

(c) Another iterative formula for the equation is:

$$x_{n+1} = \sqrt[3]{(4x_n + 2)}$$

By working out appropriate derivatives, explain why this formula will converge to the largest root from $x_1 = 2$, whereas the formula in part (b) will not.

9 (a) Given that the equation

$$x^3 - 4x^2 + 5 = 0$$

has two positive roots, find integer bounds for the larger one.

(b) Use the Newton-Raphson method to find this root correct to 4 decimal places.

(c) Use the factor theorem to find a linear factor of the left-hand side of the equation and hence solve the equation exactly.

10 The solution to a differential equation is calculated using the Runge-Kutta method. With $h = 0.2$, the value obtained is 16.4902 and with $h = 0.1$ it is 16.4552, with both values being overestimates of the actual value.

By considering the order of accuracy of the Runge-Kutta method, estimate the true value to 3 decimal places.

DIFFERENTIAL EQUATIONS

1 A small particle moves along the x-axis with acceleration given by the formula $100e^{-t-2}$, where t is time and acceleration is measured in ms^{-2}.

(a) Write the above statement as a second order differential equation in terms of distance x and time t.

(b) Find the general solution of this equation.

(c) Comment on the movement of the particle after a large period of time.

(d) Initially, the particle is at the origin and after 1000 seconds the particle's velocity is approximately 250 ms^{-1}. Find the particular solution in this case.

2 (a) Find a numerical solution to the differential equation

$$\frac{dy}{dx} = 3x \sin(1.5x^2)$$

for $0 \le x \le 2$ using a step size of 0.5 and initial value (0, 5).

(b) Now find the exact solution at $x = 2$ for the same initial value.

(c) What is the percentage error of your estimate?

3 The current i and charge q in a circuit satisfy the equations:

$$\frac{di}{dt} = -5i - 4q, \frac{dq}{dt} = i$$

Initially, $i = 0$ and $q = 3$. Using steps of $dt = 0.2$, find the current and charge at time $t = 1$.

4 For the differential equation:

$$\frac{dy}{dx} = xy(2 \ln x + 1)$$

(a) Find the general solution.

(b) Find the particular solution for which $y = 1$ when $x = 1$.

5 (a) Find the general solution of

$$\frac{dy}{dx} + 2y = e^{2x}$$

(b) Find the particular solution which passes through the origin.

6 Find the solution of

$$\frac{dy}{dx} - 2y = \cos 4x$$

which satisfies the initial condition $y = 0$ when $x = 0$.

7 The displacement x, in metres, of the top of a flag pole oscillating from side to side on a windy day is given by

$$\frac{d^2x}{dt^2} + 8\frac{dx}{dt} + 15x = 13 \sin t$$

(a) Show that $x = 0.7 \sin t - 0.4 \cos t$ is a particular solution.

(b) Find the general solution.

(c) If $x = 0$ and $\frac{dx}{dt} = 0$ when $t = 0$, calculate the displacement when $t = 1$.

8 A baby is bouncing up and down in her baby-bouncer. The oscillations are modelled by the equation:

$$\frac{d^2x}{dt^2} + 2\frac{dx}{dt} + x = 3 \cos 2t - \sin 2t$$

Given that $x = 0$ and $\frac{dx}{dt} = 0$ when $t = 0$, solve this equation of motion to find her displacement at time t.

9 In an electrical circuit, to which an alternating voltage is applied, the charge q, in coulombs, on a capacitor after t seconds is modelled by the equation:

$$\frac{d^2q}{dt^2} + 2\frac{dq}{dt} + 2q = 5 \sin 2t$$

Find expressions for the charge q, and the current in the circuit $\frac{dq}{dt}$, at time t seconds, given that both are zero when $t = 0$.

10 Two variables, x and y, satisfy the differential equations

$$\frac{dx}{dt} = x - y$$

$$\frac{dy}{dt} = y - x$$

(a) Let $u = x + y$ and $v = x - y$. Find $\frac{du}{dt}$ and $\frac{dv}{dt}$ in terms of u and v. Hence obtain the general solutions for u and v.

(b) Initially, $x = 60$ and $y = 40$. Find expressions for x and y at time t.

SOLUTIONS

MATHEMATICAL STRUCTURE

Binary operations

1

	a	b	c
a	b	c	a
b	c	a	b
c	a	b	c

Identity = c
(leaves master row and column unchanged)

2

+	0	1	2
0	0	1	2
1	1	2	0
2	2	0	1

compare to

$\circ$	c	a	b
c	c	a	b
a	a	b	c
b	b	c	a

$0 \leftrightarrow c$ (identity)
$1 \leftrightarrow a$ (or b)
$2 \leftrightarrow b$ (or a)

3

G	1	2	3	4	5
1	1	2	3	4	5
2	2	2	3	4	5
3	3	3	3	4	5
4	4	4	4	4	5
5	5	5	5	5	5

G is commutative as $a\,G\,b = b\,G\,a$ for all a, b (symmetry in leading diagonal).
Identity = 1

4 $x \sim y = |x - y|$
$y \sim x = |y - x| = |-(x - y)| = |x - y|$
i.e. commutative

$9 \sim (7 \sim 4) = 9 \sim 3 = 6$ but $(9 \sim 7) \sim 4 = 2 \sim 4 = 2$
therefore not associative

The identity is 0.

5

+	0	1	2	3	4
0	0	1	2	3	4
1	1	2	3	4	0
2	2	3	4	0	1
3	3	4	0	1	2
4	4	0	1	2	3

$\circ$	I	a	b	c	d
I	I	a	b	c	d
a	a	b	c	d	I
b	b	c	d	I	a
c	c	d	I	a	b
d	d	I	a	b	c

About centre:
a = rotate 72°
b = rotate 144°
c = rotate 216°
d = rotate 288°
I = rotate 360°

Both sets have identities (0 and I respectively).
Operations are commutative and associative.
The sets are isomorphic $0 \leftrightarrow I$, $1 \leftrightarrow a$, $2 \leftrightarrow b$, $3 \leftrightarrow c$, $4 \leftrightarrow d$. (Note that there are other isomorphisms.)

6 $a \oplus b = a + b + 1$
Identity $a \oplus e = a = a + e + 1$ therefore $e = -1$ (in set)
and $-1 \oplus a = -1 + a + 1 = a$ as required.
$a \oplus b = a + b + 1 = b + a + 1 = b \oplus a$
therefore $\oplus$ is commutative.
$a \oplus (b \oplus c) = a \oplus (b + c + 1) = a + b + c + 2$
$(a \oplus b) \oplus c = (a + b + 1) \oplus c = a + b + c + 2$
therefore $\oplus$ is associative

7 Consider $\mathrm{f}(x) = ax + b$, $\mathrm{g}(x) = cx + d$, $\mathrm{h}(x) = px + q$

$$\mathrm{f}(x) + \mathrm{g}(x) = (ax + b) + (cx + d) = (a + c)x + (b + d)$$

$$\mathrm{g}(x) + \mathrm{f}(x) = (cx + d) + (ax + b) = (c + a)x + (d + b)$$

This is commutative because $a + c = c + a$ and $b + d = d + b$ for real numbers.

$$\mathrm{f}(x) + (\mathrm{g}(x) + \mathrm{h}(x)) = (ax + b) + ((c + p)x + (d + q)) = (a + (c + p))x + (b + (d + q)) = (a + c + p)x + (b + d + q)$$

$$(\mathrm{f}(x) + \mathrm{g}(x)) + \mathrm{h}(x) = ((a + c)x + (b + d)) + (px + q) = ((a + c) + p)x + ((b + d) + q) = (a + c + p)x + (b + d + q)$$

This is associative.

f is an identity if $\mathrm{f}(x) + \mathrm{g}(x) = \mathrm{g}(x)$
$\Leftrightarrow (a + c)x + (b + d) = cx + d$
$\Leftrightarrow a = 0, b = 0$

The identity is f, where $\mathrm{f}(x) = 0$ for all x!

8 For example:
$\mathrm{f}(x) = 2x - 1$ and $\mathrm{g}(x) = 5x + 2$;
$\mathrm{fg}(x) = \mathrm{f}(5x + 2) = 2(5x + 2) - 1 = 10x + 3$
$\mathrm{gf}(x) = \mathrm{g}(2x - 1) = 5(2x - 1) + 2 = 10x - 3$

As $\mathrm{fg} \neq \mathrm{gf}$ the operation is not commutative.

Suppose $\mathrm{fg} = \mathrm{g} = \mathrm{gf}$ for $\mathrm{f}(x) = ax + b$, $\mathrm{g}(x) = cx + d$
Then $\mathrm{f}(cx + d) = cx + d$
$\Rightarrow a(cx + d) + b = cx + d$
$\Rightarrow acx + (ad + b) = cx + d$
$\Rightarrow a = 1, b = 0$

The identity is given by $\mathrm{f}(x) = x$ as you may have expected!

Set algebra

1 (a)

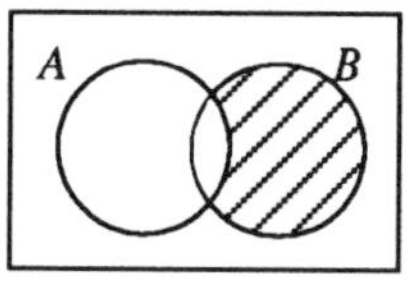

(b)

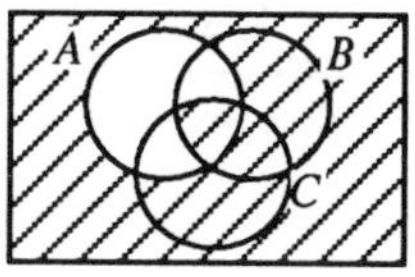

2 $(A' \cup B) \cap (A \cup B)$

$= (B \cup A') \cap (B \cup A)$	Commutative law
$= B \cup (A' \cap A)$	Distributive law
$= B \cup \varnothing$	Complement law
$= B$	Identity law

3 (a) $(A \cap B)' \cup \varepsilon$

(b) $(A \cap \varnothing) \cap (A' \cup \varepsilon)$

4

$(a \cup b')' \cap b = (a' \cap b'') \cap b$	De Morgan's law
$= (a' \cap b) \cap b$	Complement law
$= a' \cap (b \cap b)$	Associative law
$= a' \cap b$	Idempotent law

5 (a)

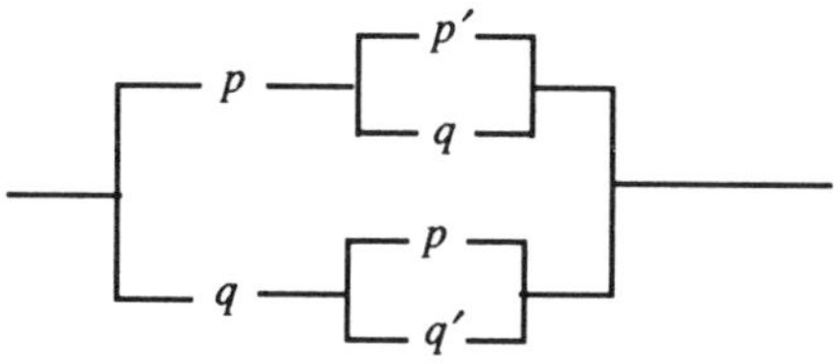

(b) $p \cap q$ —p—q—

6 (a) $a' \cup (a \cap b') \cup b'$

(b)

$= ((a' \cup a) \cap (a' \cup b')) \cup b'$	Distributive law
$= (\varepsilon \cap (a' \cup b')) \cup b'$	Complement law
$= (a' \cup b') \cup b'$	Identity law
$= a' \cup (b' \cup b')$	Associative law
$= a' \cup b'$	Idempotent law

Group theory

1 The table shows that the set is closed under this operation as only 3, 6, 9 and 12 appear. There is an identity element which is 6.

	3	6	9	12
3	9	3	12	6
6	3	6	9	12
9	12	9	6	3
12	6	12	3	9

6 and 9 are self-inverse elements. 3 and 12 are inverses of each other. Hence every element has an inverse. Since multiplication is associative this also applies to modulo 15. As the four conditions for a group are satisfied this is clearly a group.

By Lagrange's theorem subgroups must be of order 1, 2 or 4. These are {6}, {6, 9}, {6, 3, 9, 12}. The group is of order 4 so it is isomorphic to either the cyclic group $\mathbb{Z}_4$ or K. In K every element is self-inverse so this group is $\mathbb{Z}_4$. If the group table is reordered 6, 3, 9, 12, the characteristic pattern of a cyclic group appears.

By Lagrange's theorem each element must be of order 1, 2 or 4. 6 is of order 1; 3 is of order 4; 9 is of order 2; 12 is of order 4.

2 This is not a group. For example, the inverses do not all work both ways since $ad = 1$ but $da \neq 1$.

Also, associativity is not satisfied since $b(ad) = b$ but $(ba)\,d = d$.

Lagrange's theorem could also be used to justify your answer since $\{1, c\}$ forms a subgroup of order 2 which does not divide 5, the order of the containing set.

3 (i) The equilateral triangle has three lines of symmetry and therefore three reflections are possible. Call these **L**, **M** and **N**. There are two possible rotations about the centre of the triangle; one of 120° and one of 240°. Call these **R** and **R**^{2}.

The combination table is:

	I	L	M	N	R	R^2
I	I	L	M	N	R	R^2
L	L	I	R	R^2	M	N
M	M	R^2	I	R	N	L
N	N	R	R^2	I	L	M
R	R	N	L	M	R^2	I
R^2	R^2	M	N	L	I	R

N.B. The reflections are taken as follows:

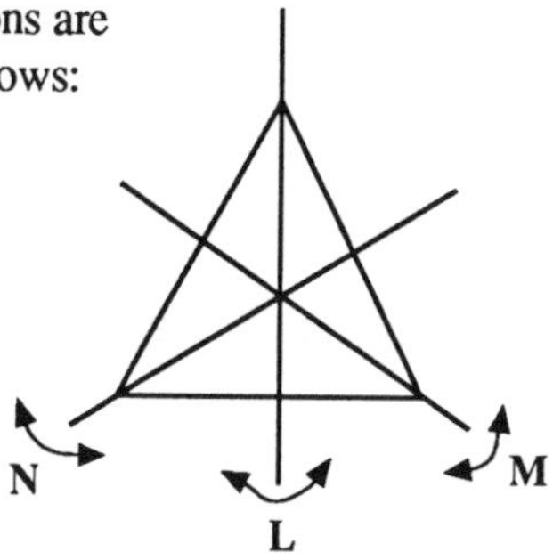

(ii) This shape has no lines of symmetry but more rotations are possible. There are six rotations (including **I**) which map the shape onto itself. Let **S** represent a rotation of 60°. The group table is then:

	I	S	S^2	S^3	S^4	S^5
I	I	S	S^2	S^3	S^4	S^5
S	S	S^2	S^3	S^4	S^5	I
S^2	S^2	S^3	S^4	S^5	I	S
S^3	S^3	S^4	S^5	I	S	S^2
S^4	S^4	S^5	I	S	S^2	S^3
S^5	S^5	I	S	S^2	S^3	S^4

The groups are not isomorphic. One way of showing this is to consider the number of self-inverse elements. The first group has 4 such elements whilst the second has only 2.

4 (a) By Fermat's Little Theorem $a^7 - a$ is divisible by 7. $a^7 - a = a(a^6 - 1)$ so a is a factor of $a^7 - a$. If a is odd then so is a^7 and $a^7 - a$ is even. Hence $a^7 - a$ is divisible by 2. Therefore the result is proved.

(b) If a is odd, $a^{11} - a$ is divisible by $22a$ for $a \neq 11n$. In general, if a is odd and p is prime $(a \neq pn)$, $a^p - a$ is divisible by $2ap$.

5 The smallest power of r which gives the identity is 4. Hence the group contains e, r, r^2 and r^3. The group also contains s, sr, sr^2 and sr^3. No further elements are generated, for example

$$\begin{aligned} r \times sr^2 &= rsr^2 \\ &= (rs)r^2 \\ &= (sr^3)r^2 \\ &= sr^5 \\ &= sr \end{aligned}$$

The group has elements $\{e, r, r^2\ r^3, s, sr, sr^2, sr^3\}$ and is of order 8. In fact, it is isomorphic to the symmetry group of the square.

6 (a) Consider any non-identity member of the group a. By Lagrange's Theorem the order of a must divide the order of the group so a is of order 5 or 25. If a is of order 5 then $\{e, a, a^2, a^3, a^4\}$ is a subgroup of order 5. If a is of order 25 then $\{e, a^5, a^{10}, a^{15}, a^{20}\}$ is the required cyclic subgroup of order 5.

(b) This follows from a similar argument to that of (a).

(c) Let a be a non-identity element. Then the order of a divides p^n and so is $p, p^2, p^3, \ldots$ or p^n. A cyclic subgroup of order p is then generated by either a, $a^p, a^{p^2}, \ldots,$ or $a^{p^{n-1}}$, respectively.

7 The subgroups must be of order 1, 2, 4 or 8 by Lagrange's Theorem. Apart from the group itself, the subgroups are isomorphic either to $\mathbb{Z}_1$, $\mathbb{Z}_2$, $\mathbb{Z}_4$ or K.

8
$$\begin{aligned} (ab)(b^{-1}a^{-1}) &= (a(bb^{-1}))a^{-1} && \text{Associativity} \\ &= (ae)a^{-1} && \text{Inverse} \\ &= aa^{-1} && \text{Identity} \\ &= e \end{aligned}$$

Hence $(ab)^{-1} = b^{-1}a^{-1}$.

9 No, for several reasons. For example, division is not associative since $6 \div (2 \div 3) = 9$ but $(6 \div 2) \div 3 = 1$.

Mathematical proof

1 The result is true when $n = 1 \Rightarrow$ P(1) is true.
Assume P(k) is true.

Then
$$\begin{aligned} &\boxed{1.1! + 2.2! + \ldots + k.k!} + (k+1)(k+1)! \\ &= (k+1)! - 1 + (k+1)(k+1)! \\ &= (k+1)!\,(1 + (k+1)) - 1 \\ &= (k+2)! - 1 \end{aligned}$$

Hence P(k + 1) is true and the proposition is true for all natural numbers n.

The remaining solutions give just part of the induction proof, starting from the assumption that P(k) is true.

2 Then
$$\begin{aligned} \frac{d}{dx}(x^{k+1}) &= \frac{d}{dx}(x.x^k) \\ &= x(kx^{k-1}) + x^k \\ &= kx^k + x^k \\ &= (k+1)x^k \end{aligned}$$

3 Assume that $k^3 - k = 3M$, so $k^3 = 3M + k$.

Then
$$\begin{aligned} &(k+1)^3 - (k+1) \\ &= k^3 + 3k^2 + 2k \\ &= (3M + k) + 3k^2 + 2k \\ &= 3M + 3k^2 + 3k \\ &= 3(M + k^2 + k) \end{aligned}$$

which is divisible by 3.

4 Then
$$\begin{aligned} &\sum_1^k r(r+1) + (k+1)(k+2) \\ &= \frac{1}{3}k(k+1)(k+2) + (k+1)(k+2) \\ &= \frac{1}{3}(k+1)(k+2)(k+3) \end{aligned}$$

5 Then
$$\begin{aligned} &\boxed{1^2 + 3^2 + 5^2 + \ldots + (2k-1)^2} + (2k+1)^2 \\ &= \frac{1}{3}k(4k^2 - 1) + (2k+1)^2 \\ &= \frac{1}{3}(k(4k^2 - 1) + 3(2k+1)^2) \\ &= \frac{1}{3}(4k^3 + 12k^2 + 11k + 3) \\ &= \frac{1}{3}(k+1)(4k^2 + 8k + 3) \\ &= \frac{1}{3}(k+1)(4(k+1)^2 - 1) \end{aligned}$$

6 Assume $4^k - 3k - 1 = 9K$, so $4^k = 9K + 3k + 1$.

Then
$$\begin{aligned} &4^{k+1} - 3(k+1) - 1 \\ &= 4.4^k - 3k - 4 \\ &= 4(9K + 3k + 1) - 3k - 4 \\ &= 36K + 9k \\ &= 9(4K + k) \end{aligned}$$

7 Then
$$\begin{aligned} &1.6 + 2.7 + \ldots + k(k+5) + (k+1)(k+6) \\ &= \frac{k}{3}(k+1)(k+8) + (k+1)(k+6) \\ &= \frac{k+1}{3}(k(k+8) + 3(k+6)) \\ &= \frac{k+1}{3}(k^2 + 11k + 18) \\ &= \frac{k+1}{3}(k+2)(k+9) \end{aligned}$$

8 Then
$$\begin{aligned} &\frac{0}{1!} + \frac{1}{2!} + \frac{2}{3!} + \ldots + \frac{k-1}{k!} + \frac{k}{(k+1)!} \\ &= 1 - \frac{1}{k!} + \frac{k}{(k+1)!} \\ &= 1 - \frac{k+1}{(k+1)!} + \frac{k}{(k+1)!} \\ &= 1 - \left[\frac{k+1-k}{(k+1)!}\right] = 1 - \frac{1}{(k+1)!} \end{aligned}$$

9 (a) $n = 41$

(b) When $a = b$, the two quantities are **equal.**

(c) The point (0, 0) on $y = |x|$.

(d) $\sqrt{2} \times \sqrt{2} = 2$

(e)

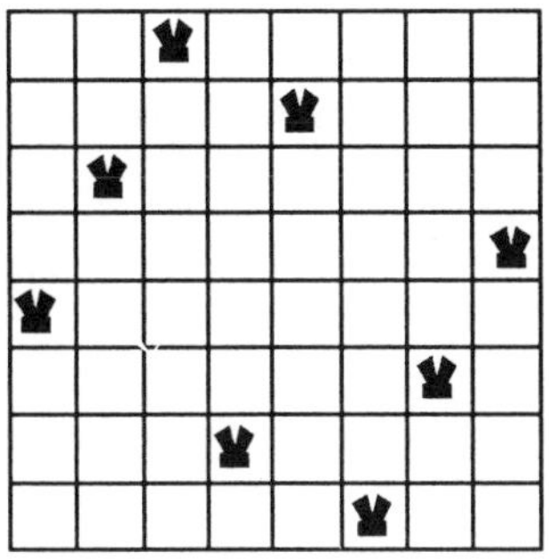

MATRICES

Introduction

1 For example, if $\mathbf{A} = \begin{bmatrix} 1 & 2 \\ 3 & 4 \end{bmatrix}$ $\mathbf{B} = \begin{bmatrix} -1 & 0 \\ 2 & 1 \end{bmatrix}$

Then $\mathbf{AB} = \begin{bmatrix} 3 & 2 \\ 5 & 4 \end{bmatrix}$ but $\mathbf{BA} = \begin{bmatrix} -1 & -2 \\ 5 & 8 \end{bmatrix}$

There are an infinity of other possible examples.

2 (a)

$$\begin{array}{c} \\ A \\ B \\ C \\ D \end{array} \begin{array}{c} \begin{matrix} A & B & C & D \end{matrix} \\ \begin{bmatrix} 4 & 1 & 0 & 0 \\ 2 & 0 & 1 & 1 \\ 1 & 1 & 2 & 1 \\ 0 & 1 & 1 & 0 \end{bmatrix} \end{array}$$

(b) (i) $\mathbf{M}^2$ represents the two-stage routes.

(ii) $\mathbf{M}^2 = \begin{bmatrix} 18 & 4 & 1 & 1 \\ 9 & 4 & 3 & 1 \\ 8 & 4 & 6 & 3 \\ 3 & 1 & 3 & 2 \end{bmatrix}$

3 (a) $\mathbf{A} + 2\mathbf{B} = \begin{bmatrix} 1 & 2 \\ 3 & 1 \end{bmatrix} + \begin{bmatrix} -2 & 0 \\ 0 & -2 \end{bmatrix} = \begin{bmatrix} -1 & 2 \\ 3 & -1 \end{bmatrix}$

(b) $\mathbf{AC} = \begin{bmatrix} 1 & 2 \\ 3 & 1 \end{bmatrix}\begin{bmatrix} 0 & 5 \\ 6 & 0 \end{bmatrix} = \begin{bmatrix} 12 & 5 \\ 6 & 15 \end{bmatrix}$

(c) $\mathbf{AB} = \begin{bmatrix} 1 & 2 \\ 3 & 1 \end{bmatrix}\begin{bmatrix} -1 & 0 \\ 0 & -1 \end{bmatrix} = \begin{bmatrix} -1 & -2 \\ -3 & -1 \end{bmatrix}$

(d) $\mathbf{CA} = \begin{bmatrix} 0 & 5 \\ 6 & 0 \end{bmatrix}\begin{bmatrix} 1 & 2 \\ 3 & 1 \end{bmatrix} = \begin{bmatrix} 15 & 5 \\ 6 & 12 \end{bmatrix}$

4 (a) $\begin{bmatrix} 0.7 & 0.5 \\ 0.3 & 0.5 \end{bmatrix}\begin{bmatrix} 1 \\ 0 \end{bmatrix} = \begin{bmatrix} 0.7 \\ 0.3 \end{bmatrix}$

So P(rain tomorrow) = 0.7

(b) $\begin{bmatrix} 0.7 & 0.5 \\ 0.3 & 0.5 \end{bmatrix}\begin{bmatrix} 0 \\ 1 \end{bmatrix} = \begin{bmatrix} 0.5 \\ 0.5 \end{bmatrix}$

So P(rain tomorrow) = 0.5

(c) $\mathbf{T}^3\begin{bmatrix} 1 \\ 0 \end{bmatrix} = \begin{bmatrix} 0.628 & 0.62 \\ 0.372 & 0.38 \end{bmatrix}\begin{bmatrix} 1 \\ 0 \end{bmatrix} = \begin{bmatrix} 0.628 \\ 0.372 \end{bmatrix}$

So P(rain in 3 days' time) = 0.628

(d) The matrix $\mathbf{T}^n$ converges to $\begin{bmatrix} 0.6 & 0.6 \\ 0.4 & 0.4 \end{bmatrix}$ as $n \to \infty$.

The probability of rain is therefore 0.6.

Matrices and transformations

1 (a) $\begin{bmatrix} 1 & 2 \\ 0 & 1 \end{bmatrix}$

(b) $\begin{bmatrix} \cos 30° & \sin 30° \\ -\sin 30° & \cos 30° \end{bmatrix} = \frac{1}{2}\begin{bmatrix} \sqrt{3} & 1 \\ -1 & \sqrt{3} \end{bmatrix}$

(c) $\begin{bmatrix} 1 & 0 \\ 0 & -1 \end{bmatrix}$

(d) $\begin{bmatrix} \cos(2\tan^{-1} 2) & \sin(2\tan^{-1} 2) \\ \sin(2\tan^{-1} 2) & -\cos(2\tan^{-1} 2) \end{bmatrix} = \begin{bmatrix} -0.6 & 0.8 \\ 0.8 & 0.6 \end{bmatrix}$

2 (a) $\begin{bmatrix} 1 & -2 \\ 0 & 1 \end{bmatrix}$ Shear
x-axis invariant, $(0, 1) \to (-2, 1)$

(b) $\frac{1}{2}\begin{bmatrix} \sqrt{3} & -1 \\ 1 & \sqrt{3} \end{bmatrix}$ Rotation 30°, anti-clockwise about the origin

(c) $\begin{bmatrix} 1 & 0 \\ 0 & -1 \end{bmatrix}$ Reflection in the x-axis (This transformation is 'self-inverse'.)

(d) $\begin{bmatrix} -0.6 & 0.8 \\ 0.8 & 0.6 \end{bmatrix}$ Reflection in $y = 2x$
(All reflections are self-inverse.)

3 (a) **S** : Reflection in x-axis
T : Rotation of 90° anti-clockwise about the origin.

(b) $\mathbf{ST}\begin{bmatrix} 1 \\ -1 \end{bmatrix} = \begin{bmatrix} 1 \\ -1 \end{bmatrix}$ Rotating $(1, -1)$ through $90° \to (1, 1)$. **Then** reflecting in x-axis gives $(1, -1)$.

(c) $\mathbf{TS}\begin{bmatrix} 1 \\ -1 \end{bmatrix} = \begin{bmatrix} -1 \\ 1 \end{bmatrix}$

(d) $\mathbf{S}^{-1} = \begin{bmatrix} 1 & 0 \\ 0 & -1 \end{bmatrix}$ Reflection in x-axis

$\mathbf{T}^{-1} = \begin{bmatrix} 0 & 1 \\ -1 & 0 \end{bmatrix}$ Rotation of 90° clockwise about the origin

4 (a) $\begin{bmatrix} 2 & 3 \\ 0 & 0 \end{bmatrix}\begin{bmatrix} x \\ y \end{bmatrix} = \begin{bmatrix} 2x+3y \\ 0 \end{bmatrix}$

All points in the plane are transformed to a point on the x-axis, and a dimension is lost.

(b) $|\mathbf{M}| = 0$. So **M** does **not** possess an inverse.

5 $\mathbf{M}_\theta^2 = \begin{bmatrix} 1 & 0 \\ 0 & 1 \end{bmatrix}$

$\mathbf{M}_\theta$ represents a reflection in the line $y = x \tan\theta$.

$\mathbf{M}_\theta^2$ represents this reflection applied twice.
A reflection is self-inverse and so $\mathbf{M}_\theta^2$ is the identity matrix representing the identity transformation.

6 **M** represents an enlargement, scale factor 2, centre the origin, together with a clockwise rotation of 60° about the origin.

7 **M** transforms the point $(x, y, z) \to (x, y, 0)$, that is, it 'squashes' 3-dimensional space onto the x–y plane.

Simultaneous equations

1 $\left(\frac{17}{11}, -\frac{10}{11}\right)$

2 $a = 6,\ b = 1$

3 $(3, 4)$

4 The lines are the same.

5 (a) $\begin{bmatrix} 2 & a \\ b & -1 \end{bmatrix}\begin{bmatrix} x \\ y \end{bmatrix} = \begin{bmatrix} 3 \\ 4 \end{bmatrix}$

$$\Rightarrow \begin{bmatrix} x \\ y \end{bmatrix} = \frac{1}{-2-ab}\begin{bmatrix} -1 & -a \\ -b & 2 \end{bmatrix}\begin{bmatrix} 3 \\ 4 \end{bmatrix}$$

$$\Rightarrow x = \frac{1}{-2-ab}(-3-4a) = \frac{3+4a}{ab+2}$$

$$y = \frac{1}{-2-ab}(-3b+8) = \frac{3b-8}{ab+2}$$

(b) x and y will be undefined if $ab + 2 = 0$.

(c) $x = \frac{15}{14},\ y = \frac{2}{7}$

6 $x = 1, y = 1, z = 2$

7 (a) $x = -\frac{3}{5},\ y = 0,\ z = \frac{4}{5}$

(b) $a = 2$

8 $(5.211, -1.684, -6.158)$ to 3 d.p.

9 $\begin{bmatrix} x \\ y \\ z \end{bmatrix} = \begin{bmatrix} 17 \\ 0 \\ -7 \end{bmatrix} + \lambda\begin{bmatrix} -1 \\ 1 \\ 1 \end{bmatrix}$

10 $-4y - 13z = -17$ ① – 3②
$-4y - 13z = -1$ 3① – ③

The original equations are inconsistent. They clearly do not represent lines and so they form a prism.

Identifying transformations

1

	Invariant points	Invariant lines (through 0)
(a)	All points on y-axis	y-axis, x-axis
(b)	Origin	Any line through 0
(c)	All points on y-axis	x-axis, y-axis

2 (a) $\begin{vmatrix} 1-\lambda & 1 \\ 4 & -2-\lambda \end{vmatrix} = 0$

$\lambda^2 + \lambda - 6 = 0$
$(\lambda + 3)(\lambda - 2) = 0$

The eigenvalues are -3 and 2.

(b) $\begin{bmatrix} 1-3 & 1 \\ 4 & -2-3 \end{bmatrix}\begin{bmatrix} x \\ y \end{bmatrix} = \begin{bmatrix} 0 \\ 0 \end{bmatrix}$

$\begin{bmatrix} 1 \\ -4 \end{bmatrix}$ is an eigenvector for $\lambda = -3$.

Similarly, $\begin{bmatrix} 1 \\ 1 \end{bmatrix}$ is an eigenvector for $\lambda = 2$.

(c) Two-way stretch, factor -3 in direction $\begin{bmatrix} 1 \\ -4 \end{bmatrix}$ and 2 in direction $\begin{bmatrix} 1 \\ 1 \end{bmatrix}$.

(d) $\mathbf{U} = \begin{bmatrix} 1 & 1 \\ -4 & 1 \end{bmatrix}$ $\mathbf{D} = \begin{bmatrix} -3 & 0 \\ 0 & 2 \end{bmatrix}$

3 $\mathbf{T} - \lambda\mathbf{I} = \begin{bmatrix} 2\sqrt{2}-\lambda & 5 \\ -1 & -\sqrt{2}-\lambda \end{bmatrix}$

So $\lambda^2 - \sqrt{2}\lambda + 1 = 0$

For this equation, '$b^2 - 4ac$' $= 2 - 4(1)(1) = -2 < 0$.
Therefore the characteristic equation has no real roots, so **T** has no eigenvalues and hence no invariant lines.

Using the Cayley-Hamilton theorem

$$\mathbf{T}^2 - \sqrt{2}\mathbf{T} + \mathbf{I} = 0$$
$$\Rightarrow \mathbf{T}^2 = \sqrt{2}\mathbf{T} - \mathbf{I}$$

Therefore $\mathbf{T}^4 = (\sqrt{2}\mathbf{T} - \mathbf{I})^2$
$= 2\mathbf{T}^2 - 2\sqrt{2}\mathbf{T} + \mathbf{I}$
$= 2(\sqrt{2}\mathbf{T} - \mathbf{I}) - 2\sqrt{2}\mathbf{T} + \mathbf{I}$
$= -\mathbf{I}$

Therefore $\mathbf{T}^4 + \mathbf{I} = 0$

4 $\mathbf{D}=\begin{bmatrix}3&0\\0&-1\end{bmatrix}$, $\mathbf{U}=\begin{bmatrix}2&1\\1&1\end{bmatrix}$, $\mathbf{U}^{-1}=\begin{bmatrix}1&-1\\-1&2\end{bmatrix}$

$$\mathbf{M}^n=\mathbf{U}\mathbf{D}^n\mathbf{U}^{-1}=\begin{bmatrix}2&1\\1&1\end{bmatrix}\begin{bmatrix}3^n&0\\0&(-1)^n\end{bmatrix}\begin{bmatrix}1&-1\\-1&2\end{bmatrix}$$

$$=3^n\begin{bmatrix}2&-2\\1&-1\end{bmatrix}+(-1)^n\begin{bmatrix}-1&2\\-1&2\end{bmatrix}$$

5 (a) $\begin{bmatrix}1\\1\end{bmatrix}$ $\begin{bmatrix}3&p\\4&q\end{bmatrix}\begin{bmatrix}1\\1\end{bmatrix}=\lambda\begin{bmatrix}1\\1\end{bmatrix}$

$\Rightarrow 3+p=\lambda$ and $4+q=\lambda$

$\Rightarrow 3+p=4+q\Rightarrow p-q=1$ ①

(b) $\begin{bmatrix}1\\-2\end{bmatrix}$ $\begin{bmatrix}3&p\\4&q\end{bmatrix}\begin{bmatrix}1\\-2\end{bmatrix}=\mu\begin{bmatrix}1\\-2\end{bmatrix}$

$\Rightarrow 2p+q=5$ ②

Solving ① and ② gives $p=2$, $q=1$.

6 $\begin{bmatrix}1&k\\4k&1\end{bmatrix}\begin{bmatrix}1\\2\end{bmatrix}=\begin{bmatrix}1+2k\\4k+2\end{bmatrix}=(1+2k)\begin{bmatrix}1\\2\end{bmatrix}$

Therefore $\begin{bmatrix}1\\2\end{bmatrix}$ is an eigenvector with eigenvalue $1+2k$.

Characteristic equation is $\lambda^2-2\lambda+(1-4k^2)=0$

$\lambda=1\pm 2k$

Therefore the other eigenvalue is $\lambda=1-2k$. The corresponding eigenvector is $\begin{bmatrix}1\\-2\end{bmatrix}$.

Numerical techniques

1 The initial equations can be reduced as shown.

x_1	x_2	x_3	x_4	c	
0	−2	4	−0.5	−8	③ − 0.5 ①
0	1	1	−4	−19	② − ①
0	1	3	−0.5	−9	④ − 0.5 ①

The eventual solution is $x_1=1$, $x_2=-1$, $x_3=-2$, $x_4=4$.

2 $x_1=1$, $x_2=2$, $x_3=5$

3 Let $\begin{bmatrix}1&0&0\\a&1&0\\b&c&1\end{bmatrix}\begin{bmatrix}d&e&f\\0&g&h\\0&0&i\end{bmatrix}=\begin{bmatrix}2&1&1\\1&4&2\\2&-1&5\end{bmatrix}$

Then $d=2$, $e=1$, $f=1$, $ad=1\Rightarrow a=0.5$,

$ae+g=4\Rightarrow g=3.5$, $af+h=2\Rightarrow h=1.5$,

$bd=2\Rightarrow b=1$, $be+cg=-1\Rightarrow c=-\frac{4}{7}$

$bf+ch+i=5\Rightarrow i=\frac{34}{7}$

$$\begin{bmatrix}1&0&0\\\frac{1}{2}&1&0\\1&-\frac{4}{7}&1\end{bmatrix}\begin{bmatrix}y_1\\y_2\\y_3\end{bmatrix}=\begin{bmatrix}1\\-11\\10\end{bmatrix}\Rightarrow\begin{bmatrix}y_1\\y_2\\y_3\end{bmatrix}=\begin{bmatrix}1\\-\frac{23}{2}\\\frac{17}{7}\end{bmatrix}$$

$$\begin{bmatrix}2&1&1\\0&\frac{7}{2}&\frac{3}{2}\\0&0&\frac{34}{7}\end{bmatrix}\begin{bmatrix}x_1\\x_2\\x_3\end{bmatrix}=\begin{bmatrix}1\\-\frac{23}{2}\\\frac{17}{7}\end{bmatrix}\Rightarrow\begin{bmatrix}x_1\\x_2\\x_3\end{bmatrix}=\begin{bmatrix}2\\-3.5\\0.5\end{bmatrix}$$

4 $$\begin{bmatrix}1&0&0\\0.2&1&0\\0.6&-2&1\end{bmatrix}\begin{bmatrix}5&2&1\\0&2.6&1.8\\0&0&8\end{bmatrix}\begin{bmatrix}x_1\\x_2\\x_3\end{bmatrix}=\begin{bmatrix}5\\-2.5\\-14.8\end{bmatrix}$$

$$\Rightarrow\quad\begin{bmatrix}5&2&1\\0&2.6&1.8\\0&0&8\end{bmatrix}\begin{bmatrix}x_1\\x_2\\x_3\end{bmatrix}=\begin{bmatrix}5\\-3.5\\-24.8\end{bmatrix}$$

$$\Rightarrow\quad\begin{bmatrix}x_1\\x_2\\x_3\end{bmatrix}=\begin{bmatrix}1.3\\0.8\\-3.1\end{bmatrix}$$

5 $$\begin{bmatrix}1&0&0\\0.4&1&0\\0.2&-2&1\end{bmatrix}\begin{bmatrix}5&4&2\\0&-3.6&2.2\\0&0&7\end{bmatrix}\begin{bmatrix}x_1\\x_2\\x_3\end{bmatrix}=\begin{bmatrix}6\\-2\\-10\end{bmatrix}$$

$$\Rightarrow\quad\begin{bmatrix}5&4&2\\0&-3.6&2.2\\0&0&7\end{bmatrix}\begin{bmatrix}x_1\\x_2\\x_3\end{bmatrix}=\begin{bmatrix}6\\-12.4\\-28\end{bmatrix}$$

$$\Rightarrow\quad\begin{bmatrix}x_1\\x_2\\x_3\end{bmatrix}=\begin{bmatrix}2\\1\\-4\end{bmatrix}$$

6 $x_{n+1}=\dfrac{9+3y_n}{8}$, $y_{n+1}=\dfrac{79-3z_n}{20}$,

$z_{n+1}=\dfrac{-73+x_{n+1}}{10}$, with starting values $x_1=0$, $y_1=0$, $z_1=0$, lead to the solution $x=3$, $y=5$, $z=-7$.

7 $w_{n+1}=\dfrac{43.8-x_n}{8}$, $x_{n+1}=\dfrac{22.6-y_n}{10}$,

$y_{n+1}=\dfrac{8.8-z_n}{8}$, $z_{n+1}=\dfrac{9.6+2w_{n+1}}{5}$, with

starting values $x_1=y_1=z_1=w_1=0$, lead to the solution $w=5.2$, $x=2.2$, $y=0.6$, $z=4.0$.

8 $5.55x+3y=96$
$13.55x+7.4y=237.2$
has solution set $x=-2.85714$, $y=37.2857$

$5.45x+3y=96$
$13.65x+7.4y=237.2$
has solution set $x=1.93548$, $y=28.4839$

The equations are therefore ill-conditioned.

9 (a) Solution set for $3.225x + 4.183y = 115.9$, $6.386x - 8.246y = -101.1$

is $x = 9.99531$, $y = 20.0012$

Solution set for $3.2x + 4.2y = 115.9$, $6.4x - 8.2y = -101.1$

is $x = 9.89759$, $y = 20.0542$

The equations are relatively well-conditioned because the gradients of the two lines are quite different.

(b) Solution set for $3.225x + 4.183y = 115.9$, $6.386x + 8.246y = -101.1$

is $x = -11557$, $y = 8938$

Solution set for $3.2x + 4.2y = 115.9$, $6.4x + 8.2y = -101.1$

is $x = -2148.4$, $y = 1664.5$

The equations are ill-conditioned. Note that the gradients of the two lines are almost equal.

Canonical form

1 (a) $\begin{bmatrix} 3 & 1 & 0 & 2 \\ 1 & -3 & -2 & -6 \\ 1 & 2 & 1 & 4 \end{bmatrix}$

(b) 3② − ①, 3③ − ① $\Rightarrow \begin{bmatrix} 3 & 1 & 0 & 2 \\ 0 & -10 & -6 & -20 \\ 0 & 5 & 3 & 10 \end{bmatrix}$

10① + ②, 2③ + ② $\Rightarrow \begin{bmatrix} 30 & 0 & -6 & 0 \\ 0 & -10 & -6 & -20 \\ 0 & 0 & 0 & 0 \end{bmatrix}$

$\frac{1}{30}$①, $-\frac{1}{10}$② $\Rightarrow \begin{bmatrix} 1 & 0 & -\frac{1}{5} & 0 \\ 0 & 1 & \frac{3}{5} & 2 \\ 0 & 0 & 0 & 0 \end{bmatrix}$

(c) $\mathbf{k} = \lambda \begin{bmatrix} 1 \\ -3 \\ 5 \end{bmatrix}$ (d) $\mathbf{p} = \begin{bmatrix} 0 \\ 2 \\ 0 \end{bmatrix}$

(e) $\mathbf{r} = \begin{bmatrix} 0 \\ 2 \\ 0 \end{bmatrix} + \lambda \begin{bmatrix} 1 \\ -3 \\ 5 \end{bmatrix}$

2 (a) $\mathbf{k} = \lambda \begin{bmatrix} -4 \\ 7 \\ 5 \\ 0 \end{bmatrix} + \mu \begin{bmatrix} -3 \\ -1 \\ 0 \\ 5 \end{bmatrix}$ (b) 2

(c) $\begin{bmatrix} 2.6 \\ -0.8 \\ 0 \\ 0 \end{bmatrix} + \lambda \begin{bmatrix} -4 \\ 7 \\ 5 \\ 0 \end{bmatrix} + \mu \begin{bmatrix} -3 \\ -1 \\ 0 \\ 5 \end{bmatrix}$

3 $\mathbf{r} = \begin{bmatrix} 1 \\ 0 \\ 0 \end{bmatrix} + \lambda \begin{bmatrix} 1 \\ 2 \\ 1 \end{bmatrix}$

4 $\left[\begin{array}{ccc|c} 1 & 0 & -0.5 & 0.5 \\ 0 & 1 & 0.25 & -1.75 \\ 0 & 0 & 0 & -2 \end{array}\right]$ This number is not zero and so there is no solution.

5 (a) $a \neq 4$ (b) (i) $a \neq 4, b \neq 9$

(b) (ii) $a = 4, b = 9$

$\mathbf{r} = \begin{bmatrix} 5.8 \\ 2.6 \\ 0 \end{bmatrix} + \lambda \begin{bmatrix} -11 \\ -2 \\ 5 \end{bmatrix}$

COMPLEX NUMBERS

Complex number geometry

1 (a) $7 + 3j$ (b) $28 + 24j$ (c) $16 - 30j$

2 $5 \pm 2j$

3 $1 - \sqrt{3}j = [2, -60°]$
$(1 - \sqrt{3}j)^5 = [32, -300°] = 16 + 16\sqrt{3}j$

4 $z = 5 - 4j, w = 1 + j$

5 $[1, -60°]^4 - [1, 60°]^4 = [1, 120°] - [1, -120°]$
$= \sqrt{3}j$

6 $(1 + cj)^3 = (1 - 3c^2) + (3c - c^3)j$
$\Rightarrow 3c - c^3 = 0$ as z^3 is real.
So $c = 0, \pm\sqrt{3}$ and $z = 1$ or $1 \pm \sqrt{3}j$.

7 $-11 + 27j$

8 $x = a \pm 2bj$

9 (a) $z^4 = [64, 180°]$ (b) $\frac{z^4}{w} = [32\sqrt{2}, 135°]$

(c) $\frac{1}{z} = [\frac{1}{\sqrt{8}}, 45°]$

10 (a) $\sin(90° + \theta) = \sin 90° \cos\theta + \cos 90° \sin\theta = \cos\theta$
$\cos(90° + \theta) = \cos 90° \cos\theta - \sin 90° \sin\theta = -\sin\theta$

(b) $jz = r(j\cos\theta + j^2 \sin\theta)$
$= r(-\sin\theta + j\cos\theta)$
$= r(\cos(90° + \theta) + j\sin(90° + \theta))$
$= [r, 90° + \theta]$, as required.

11 (a) $\frac{5}{2}(-\sqrt{3} + j)$ (b) $[\sqrt{10}, 108.4°]$

12 (a) $zw = \frac{16}{5}(-4 + 3j)$ (b) $z^2 = \frac{4}{25}(7 + 24j)$

Complex number algebra

1 (a) $z^* = 4 - 3j$

(b) $zz^* = 25,\ z + z^* = 8$

2 (a) $z^2 = -4 \Rightarrow z = \pm 2j$

(b) $z = \dfrac{2 \pm \sqrt{(4-8)}}{2} = \dfrac{2 \pm \sqrt{-4}}{2} = \dfrac{2 \pm 2j}{2} = 1 \pm j$

(c) $(z-3)(z^2 + 4z - 5) = 0$
$(z-3)(z+5)(z-1) = 0$
Therefore solutions are $z = 3, -5, 1$.

(d) Since coefficients are real, $-3 - 2j$ is another root. These roots give the quadratic $z^2 + 6z + 13 = 0$ so the other factor is $(z + 2)$. The solutions are -2, $-3 \pm 2j$.

3 (a) $z^2 - 2z + 10 = 0$

(b) $z^2 + 4 = 0$

(c) $(z-1)(z-j) = 0$ or $z^2 - (1+j)z + j = 0$

4 Quadratic with roots $1 \pm 2j$ is $z^2 - 2z + 5 = 0$
$\Rightarrow (z^2 - 2z + 5)(z - 3) = z^3 - 5z^2 + 11z - 15 = 0$

5 (a) j (b) $\dfrac{5}{13} - \dfrac{12}{13}j$ (c) $3 - 2j$

6 The roots give $(z - 2j)(z^2 - 9)$. Therefore the coefficient of z^2 is $a = -2j$.

7 $(\sqrt{2} + j)^{-6} = \left[\sqrt{3}, \tan^{-1}\dfrac{1}{\sqrt{2}}\right]^{-6} = \left[3^{-3}, -6\tan^{-1}\dfrac{1}{\sqrt{2}}\right]$
$= [3^{-3}, 3.693] = -0.032 - 0.019j$

8 (a) $[r, \theta]^4 = \left[1, \dfrac{\pi}{2}\right] \Rightarrow r^4 = 1, 4\theta = \dfrac{\pi}{2} + 2\pi n$

$\Rightarrow \left(1, \dfrac{\pi}{8}\right), \left(1, \dfrac{5\pi}{8}\right), \left(1, \dfrac{9\pi}{8}\right), \left(1, \dfrac{13\pi}{8}\right)$

(b) $r^3 = \sqrt{2},\ 3\theta = 45° + 360n°$

$\Rightarrow [2^{1/6}, 15°], [2^{1/6}, 135°], [2^{1/6}, 255°]$

(c) If $z + 1 = w$, $w^3 = 1 + j$ has been solved in (b), therefore subtract 1 from each solution i.e. $2^{1/6}(\cos 15° + j \sin 15°) - 1$ etc.

9 $z^3 = -27 \Rightarrow [r^3, 3\theta] = [27, 180° + 360n°]$
$\Rightarrow r = 3, \theta = 60°, 180°, 300°$
$\Rightarrow z = 1.5 \pm 2.6j, -3.$

10 $z^4 = 1 - j \Rightarrow [r^4, 4\theta] = [\sqrt{2}, -45° + 360n°]$
$\Rightarrow r = 2^{1/8},\ \theta = -\dfrac{45}{4}^\circ, \dfrac{315}{4}^\circ, \dfrac{675}{4}^\circ, \dfrac{1035}{4}^\circ$

11 The solutions are 0 and $-j$.

12 $z^2 = 25j$.

Loci

1 (a)

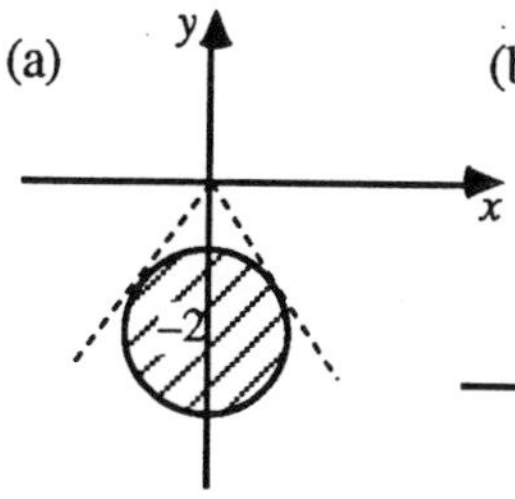

(b)

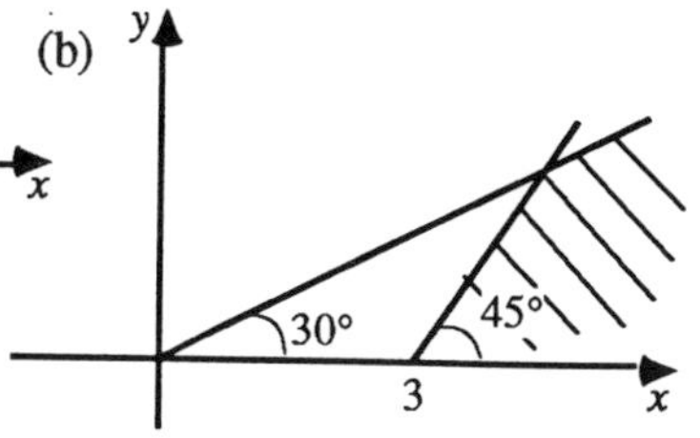

(c)

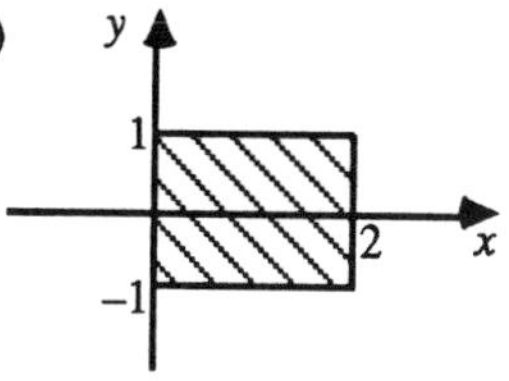

2 $1 \le |z| \le 3$ $\quad -120° \le \arg(z) \le -60°$

3

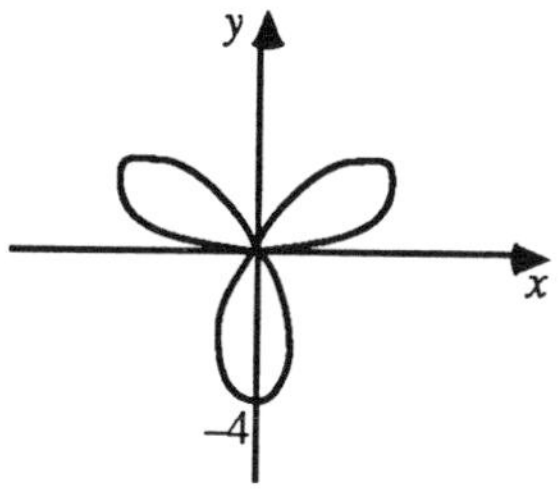

4 $\{\omega : \arg(\omega) = 120°\}$

5 (a) $\omega = z(1 - j) \Rightarrow z = \dfrac{\omega}{1-j}$

$|z - 1 - 4j| < 2 \Rightarrow \left|\dfrac{\omega}{1-j} - 1 - 4j\right| < 2$

$\Rightarrow |\omega - 5 - 3j| < 2\sqrt{2}$

(b) The interior of a circle, radius $2\sqrt{2}$, centre $5 + 3j$.

6 (a) Enlargement, scale factor 2, centre 0, followed by a translation $\begin{bmatrix} 0 \\ -1 \end{bmatrix}$

(b) Translation $\begin{bmatrix} 0 \\ -1 \end{bmatrix}$ followed by an anti-clockwise rotation through 90° about the origin

(c) Translation $\begin{bmatrix} 1 \\ -3 \end{bmatrix}$ followed by a reflection in the real axis

(d) Reflection in the imaginary axis followed by a translation $\begin{bmatrix} 0 \\ 2 \end{bmatrix}$

7 (a) $2|x + jy| = |x - 3 + jy|$
$\Rightarrow 4[x^2 + y^2] = [(x-3)^2 + y^2]$
$\Rightarrow (x+1)^2 + y^2 = 4$

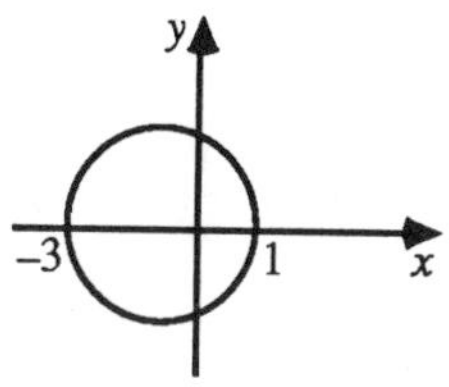

(b) Centre $(-1, 0)$, radius 2

8 The locus is a semi-circle with the line joining $0 \to 3j$ as diameter.

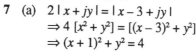

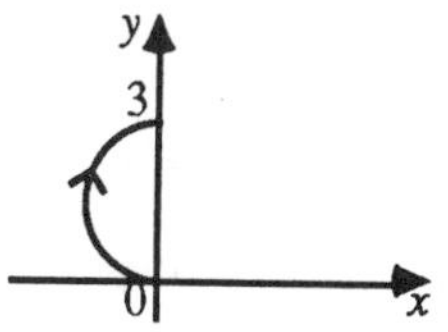

The exponential function

1 (a) $-\frac{1}{\sqrt{2}} + \frac{1}{\sqrt{2}}j$ (b) $0.046 + 0.246j$

(c) $0.531 + 3.59j$ (d) $0.347 + (5.50 + 2n\pi)j$

2

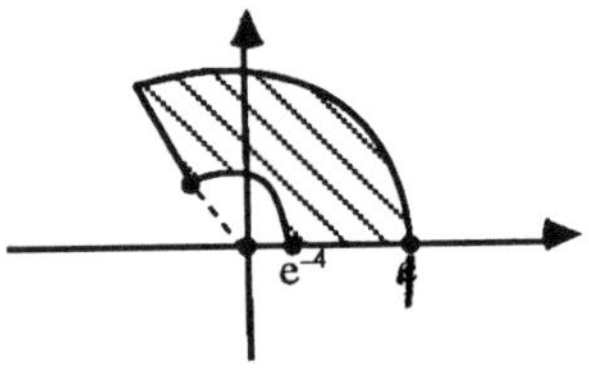

Angle = 2^c

3 $\ln(\sqrt{3} + j) = 0.693 + (0.524 + 2n\pi)j$

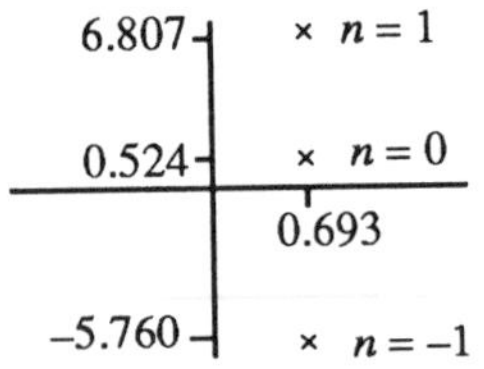

4 $\ln\left(\frac{z_1}{z_2}\right) = \ln\left(\frac{r_1}{r_2} e^{j(\theta_1 - \theta_2)}\right)$

$= \ln\left(\frac{r_1}{r_2}\right) + j(\theta_1 - \theta_2) + 2n\pi j$

$= \ln(z_1) - \ln(z_2)$

5 $\frac{1}{2}(e^{jz} + e^{-jz}) = -2$

$e^{jz} = -2 \pm \sqrt{3}$

$z = \pi + 2n\pi - j\ln(2 \pm \sqrt{3})$

6 $X + jY = \cos x \cos j - \sin x \sin j$

So $\left(\frac{X}{a}\right)^2 + \left(\frac{Y}{b}\right)^2 = 1$, where

$a = \frac{1}{2}(e + e^{-1})$ and $b = \frac{1}{2}(e - e^{-1})$

7 $z = (-2)^{1/4} = e^{1/4 \ln(-2)}$

$z = \pm 0.84(1 + j)$ or $\pm 0.84(1 - j)$

8 (a) $\sin^2 z + \cos^2 z$

$= -\frac{1}{4}(e^{2jz} - 2 + e^{-2jz}) + \frac{1}{4}(e^{2jz} + 2 + e^{-2jz})$

$= 1$

(b) $\cos t \cos z + \sin t \sin z$

$= \frac{1}{4}(e^{jt} + e^{-jt})(e^{jz} + e^{-jz}) - \frac{1}{4}(e^{jt} - e^{-jt})(e^{jz} - e^{-jz})$

$= \frac{1}{2}(e^{-j(t-z)} + e^{j(t-z)})$

$= \cos(t - z)$

9 $\cos z = \frac{1}{2}(e^{jz} + e^{-jz})$

$= \frac{1}{2}[(1 + jz + \ldots) + (1 - jz + \ldots)]$

$= 1 - \frac{z^2}{2!} + \frac{z^4}{4!} - \ldots$

For sin z, similarly use $\frac{1}{2j}(e^{jz} - e^{-jz})$.

10 (a) $\sqrt{10}\, e^{1.25j}$ (b) $\sqrt{2}\, e^{(5\pi/4)j}$

Further transformations

1 (a) $-j, j$ (b) $\frac{1}{2}(j - 1), -\frac{1}{2}(j + 1)$

2

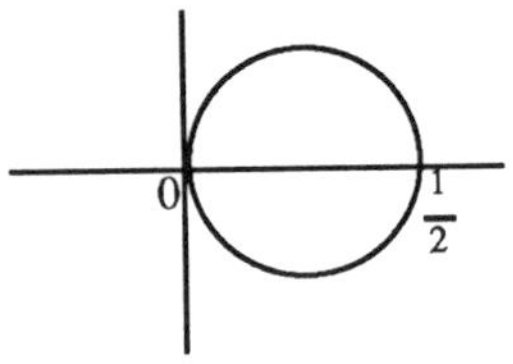

3

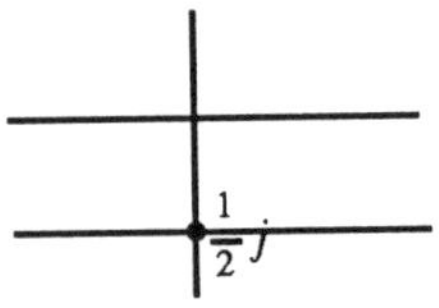

4 $\left|\omega - \frac{2}{3}\right| = \frac{2}{3}|\omega|$

5 (a) $1 + \frac{7}{z - 2}$ (b) $2 + \frac{5}{z - 2}$

(c) $\frac{1}{2} - \frac{3}{4z + 2}$ (d) $j + \frac{2}{z + 3}$

6 translation $\begin{bmatrix} 3 \\ 0 \end{bmatrix}$, inversion, enlargement factor 2,

translation $\begin{bmatrix} 0 \\ 1 \end{bmatrix}$

7

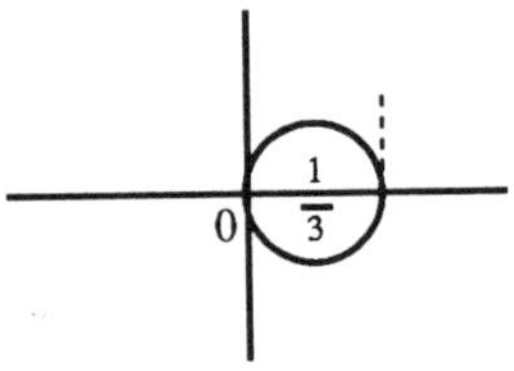

circle centre $\frac{1}{3}$
radius $\frac{1}{3}$

8 (a) $1 \to 2, \quad -1 \to -2, \quad \pm j \to 0$

(b) $\left|z + \frac{1}{z}\right| = \left|\frac{z^2 + 1}{z}\right| = \frac{|z^2 + 1|}{|z|} \leq \frac{1 + 1}{1} = 2$

9 (a)

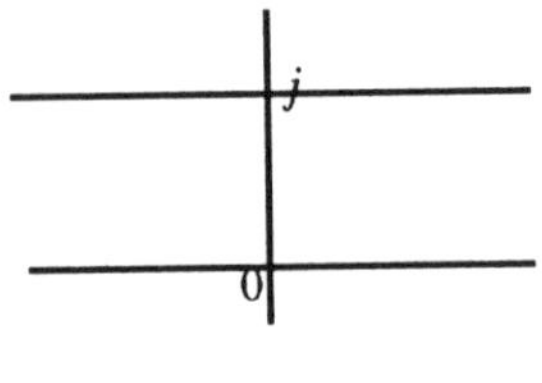

$y = j$

(b)

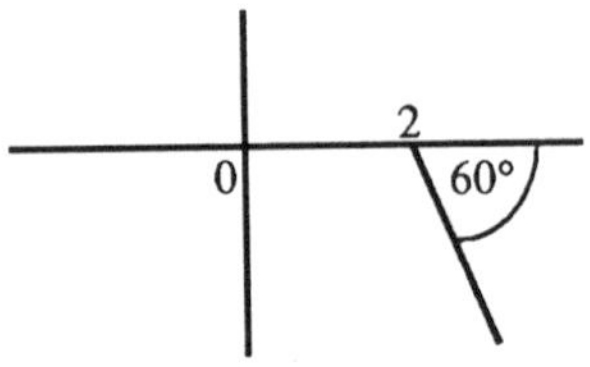

$\arg(z - 2) = -\frac{\pi}{3}$

Towards chaos

1 $1, 2j, -2+j, -1-j$

2 (a) 1 (b) 0, 1 (c) 3, –2 (d) $j, -2j$

3 $z_1 = j,\ z_2 = 0,\ z_3 = 1,\ z_4 = 1+j,$ so the order is 4.

4 $z_{n+1} = \left[1, \dfrac{2\pi}{5}\right] z_n$

5 Any fixed points must be in the set. These are –2, 3. 2, –3 are also in the set.

6 For –2, the iterations give 0, –2, 2, 2, ... so the orbit of 0 does not go to infinity.
For 2, you obtain 0, 2, 6, 38 ... which tends to infinity.

7 $z_1 = -a + j$

$z_2 = a(a^2-2) - j(2a^2-1)$

8 j

9 $z_1 = b = j$

$z_2 = -a + j = -1 + j$

$\Rightarrow a = 1$

$\Rightarrow z_3 = -j,\ z_4 = j - 1$ so the period is of order 2.

NUMERICAL METHODS

Errors

1 (a) $\left(\dfrac{0.01}{2.16} + \dfrac{0.01}{1.24} + \dfrac{0.01}{3.08}\right) \times 2 = 0.032$

(b) 0.064 (double the relative error for (a))

(c) 0.016 (half the relative error for (a))

2 (a) Relative error is $\dfrac{0.25}{50} + 2\,\dfrac{0.1}{1.4} = 0.15$
Range of values is $10.07\,(1 \pm 0.15)$
So $8.56 \le g \le 11.58$.

(b) Time for one swing is now 1.42 ± 0.01 seconds, so the relative error is $\dfrac{0.25}{50} + 2\,\dfrac{0.01}{1.42} = 0.019$
Range of values is $9.79\,(1 \pm 0.019)$

$9.60 \le g \le 9.98$.

3 (a) $d = 8.37 \times 10^5$

(b) Relative error

$$= \left[2\,\frac{0.005}{6.36} + \frac{0.005}{9.81} + 2\,\frac{0.005}{2.60}\right] \div 3 = 0.00198$$

So the maximum error is approximately 0.2%.

4 Relative error

$$= \left[\frac{0.05}{3.1} + \frac{0.05}{2.4} + \frac{1}{2}\left(\frac{0.5}{41}\right)\right] \times 3 = 0.129$$

So the maximum error is approximately 13%.

5 (a) (i) $39 = 100111_2$

(ii) $4.1 = 100.000110011001100\ldots_2$

(b) $13 = \dfrac{13}{16} \times 16 = 0.1101_2 \times 2^4$

6 $10^2 \times 10^{-3} = 10^{-1}$
So $10^4 \times b < 10^{-1}$
$b < 10^{-5}$

7 To 8 s.f., $e^1 = 2.7182818$, $e^{1+10^{-5}} = 2.7183090$, $e^{1+10^{-6}} = 2.7182845$

(a) Each of the values above is correct to $\pm 5 \times 10^{-8}$.

$e^{1+10^{-5}} - e^1 = 2.72 \times 10^{-5} \pm (2 \times 5 \times 10^{-8})$
$= (2.72 \pm 0.01) \times 10^{-5}$

Dividing by 10^{-5} gives a gradient of 2.72 ± 0.01.

The gradient of e^x at $x = 1$ is 2.71828 ... = e. This is in the required range.

(b) The second answer is 2.7 ± 0.1. The relative error for the difference between $e^{1+10^{-6}}$ and e^1 is high because the limit of accuracy of the calculator is being reached.

Areas

1 $h = 0.125$ gives 3.19459686.

$$\int_0^1 e^{2x}\,dx = \left[\tfrac{1}{2}e^{2x}\right]_0^1 = 3.194528049$$

Error $= 2.15 \times 10^{-3}\%$

2 $h = \dfrac{\pi}{8}$ gives 246.7401101 cm³.

$$\pi \int_0^{\pi/2} 100 \sin^2 x\,dx = 100\pi \left[\frac{x}{2} - \frac{1}{4}\sin 2x\right]_0^{\pi/2}$$

$= 246.7401101$ cm³, the same.

3 Simpson's rule gives

$$\frac{0.5}{3}\left[0 + 8 + 4\left(\frac{1}{8} + \frac{27}{8}\right) + 2 \times 1\right] = 4$$

$$\int_0^2 x^3\,dx = \left[\frac{x^4}{4}\right]_0^2 = 4$$

So Simpson's rule gives the exact answer.

4 $V = \pi \int_a^b x^2 \, dy$. $y = e^x \Rightarrow x = \ln y$ and the limits are $e^0 = 1$ and $e^1 = e$. $h = \dfrac{e - 1}{6}$ gives 2.257151428.

5 $A_F = 1.27589$, $A_L = 1.70546$, $A_M = 1.44875$, $A_T = 1.49068$, $A_S = 1.46272$

It is now easy to check that (a), (b) and (c) are all satisfied.

6 Exact value $= \int_0^1 e^x \, dx = e^1 - 1$.

n	Simpson's rule	error
2	1.71886115	5.8×10^{-4}
4	1.71831884	3.7×10^{-5}
8	1.71828415	2.3×10^{-6}

Error for $n = 2 \approx 2^4 \times$ error for $n = 4$.
Error for $n = 4 \approx 2^4 \times$ error for $n = 8$.

So Simpson's rule is fourth order.

7 Using $h = 1$, $A = 6170$ kg ms^{-1}.

Taylor polynomials

1 (a) $f'(2) = \dfrac{f(2.1) - f(2)}{0.1} = -1.118206$

(b) $f'(2) = \dfrac{f(2.1) - f(1.9)}{2(0.1)} = -1.027017$

The actual value of the gradient of $y = e^{\sin x}$ at $x = 2$ is $\cos 2 \, e^{\sin 2} \approx -1.033$.

The absolute errors are

	$h = 0.1$	$h = 0.01$	$h = 0.001$
First approx.	0.08509	0.00908	0.000913
Second approx.	0.0061	0.000061	0.00000062

It can be seen from the table that the first approximation has first order accuracy while the second approximation has second order accuracy.

2 $f(1) = f'(1) = f''(1) = e$

$$f(x) \approx f(1) + f'(1)[x - 1] + f''(1)\left[\frac{(x-1)^2}{2!}\right]$$

$$\Rightarrow f(x) \approx e + e(x - 1) + \frac{e}{2}(x - 1)^2$$

$$\approx \frac{e}{2}(x^2 + 1)$$

Whereas Taylor's first approximation is tangential to the original function, the second approximation matches the function more closely and is therefore 'better'.

3 $S(0) = 0$, $S'(0) = 1$, $S''(0) = 0$, $S^{(3)}(0) = -1$, $S^{(4)}(0) = 0$, $S^{(5)}(0) = 1$

So $s(x) = 0 + x + 0 - \dfrac{x^3}{3!} + 0 + \dfrac{x^5}{5!}$

$= x - \dfrac{1}{6}x^3 + \dfrac{1}{120}x^5$

For small x, $s(x)$ is an excellent approximation to $\sin x$.

4 $\cos x = 1 - \dfrac{x^2}{2!} + \dfrac{x^4}{4!} - \dfrac{x^6}{6!} + \ldots$ for all x

Replace x by $3x$ to give:

$\cos 3x = 1 - \dfrac{9x^2}{2} + \dfrac{81x^4}{24} - \dfrac{729x^6}{720} + \ldots$ for all x

5 $y' = 2x e^{x^2} = 2xy \Rightarrow y'' = 2xy' + 2y$
$\Rightarrow y^{(3)} = 2(2y' + xy'')$

Then $y^{(4)} = 2(3y'' + xy^{(3)})$
$y^{(5)} = 2(4y^{(3)} + xy^{(4)})$
$y^{(6)} = 2(5y^{(4)} + xy^{(5)})$

$y(0) = 1$, $y'(0) = 0$, $y''(0) = 2$, $y^{(3)}(0) = 0$;
$y^{(4)}(0) = 12$, $y^{(5)}(0) = 0$, $y^{(6)} = 120$

So $y = e^{x^2} = 1 + x^2 + \dfrac{x^4}{2} + \dfrac{x^6}{6} + \ldots$

Replace x by $2x$ in this series:

$$e^{4x^2} = 1 + 4x^2 + 8x^4 + \frac{32x^6}{3} + \ldots$$

Solving equations

1 (a) $[-3, -2]$, $[-1, 0]$, $[2, 3]$

(b) One root in $[-2, -1]$ and two in $[0, 1]$. Note that $f(0)$ and $f(1)$ are both positive, but $f(0.5)$ is negative.

2 $f'(x) = 3x^2 + 2$, so the gradient of $y = f(x)$ is always positive. $f(x)$ is continuous and so has no more than one real root. $f(1) = -2$, $f(2) = 7$, so the root is in $[1, 2]$. $x = 1.33$. Decimal search needs 8 more calculations than bisection.

3 (a) $x^4 = 3x - 1$, $x = \sqrt[4]{(3x - 1)}$

(b) $x^4 = 3x - 1$, $x^3 = 3 - \dfrac{1}{x}$

$x = \sqrt[3]{(3 - \dfrac{1}{x})}$

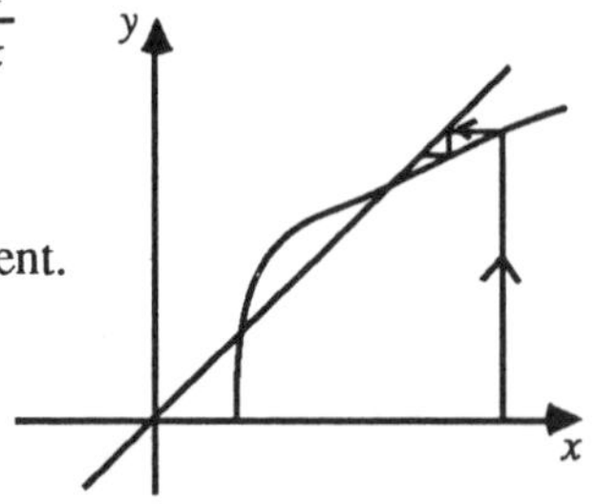

Formula (b) is more efficient.

At the root, $x \approx 1.31$:

(a) $g'(x) = 0.33$
(b) $g'(x) = 0.11$

4 (a) 58 (b) 5 (on the author's calculator)

5 6.6702

6 f(0) = –0.099999, f(1) = 0.930301. 21 iterations are needed because the stationary point on $y = f(x)$ is close to $x = 0$.

7 f(1) = –3, f(2) = 2. $f'(1.5) \approx \dfrac{f(1.50001) - f(1.5)}{0.00001} \approx 4.36$. $x_2 \approx 1.69$.

8 Two roots in $[0, 2\pi]$, two in $[2\pi, 4\pi]$, and so on until $\ln x > 4$, i.e. $x > e^4 \approx 17.4\pi$, so there is only one root in $[16\pi, 18\pi]$. Total = 17. $x = 1.4737$.

Differential equations

1 (a) (2, –1), (2.2, 9.92), (2.4, 35.21), (2.6, 98.68), (2.8, 271.21), (3.0, 779.25)

f(3) ≈ 779

(b) The graph is concave upwards and so you would expect the estimate to be less than the correct value.

2 (a) Midpoint Euler

(0, 0), (0.1, –0.0001), (0.2, –0.001), (0.3, –0.004), (0.4, –0.0106666968)

Improved Euler

(0,0), (0.1, –0.0003), (0.2, –0.0015), (0.3, –0.0048), (0.4, –0.01119492941)

(b) Runge-Kutta

(0,0), (0.1, –0.0002), (0.2, –0.0013) (0.3, –0.0045), (0.4, –0.01084277434)

(c) $\dfrac{(2 \times -0.0106666968) - 0.01119492941}{3}$

≈ -0.01084277434

3 (a) You cannot start from (0, 3) because the gradient is infinite between $x = 0$ and $x = 2$.

(b) (3, 5), (3.25, 4.97), (3.5, 4.95), (3.75, 4.93) (4.0, 4.908536598).

f(4) ≈ 4.909

(c) $\dfrac{1}{1-x^2} = \dfrac{1}{2(1-x)} + \dfrac{1}{2(1+x)}$

$$\int_3^4 \frac{1}{1-x^2}\,dx = \left[\frac{1}{2}\ln|1+x| - \frac{1}{2}\ln|1-x|\right]_3^4$$

$$= \frac{1}{2}\ln\left(\frac{5}{6}\right)$$

$$f(4) = 5 + \frac{1}{2}\ln\left(\frac{5}{6}\right)$$

4 (a) Euler's method

(1, 2), (1.5, 3.5), (2.0, 6.875), (2.5, 12.875), (3.0, 22.25)

(b) Improved Euler

(1, 2), (1.5, 4.4375), (2.0, 9.125), (2.5, 16.8125), (3.0, 28.25)

(c) Runge-Kutta

(1, 2), (1.5, 4.375), (2.0, 9), (2.5, 16.625), (3.0, 28)

(d) $\displaystyle\int_1^3 3x^2\,dx = \left[x^3\right]_1^3 = 26$

f(3) = 2 + 26 = 28

DIFFERENTIAL EQUATIONS

Review

1 (a) (i) $\dfrac{d^3y}{dx^3} = 5^3e^{5x}$ (ii) $\dfrac{d^ny}{dx^n} = 5^ne^{5x}$

(b) $\dfrac{d^ny}{dx^n} = \dfrac{(-1)^{n+1}(n-1)!}{x^n}$

2 $\dfrac{d^2y}{dx^2} = \omega^2\cos\omega x$, so $\dfrac{d^2y}{dx^2} = -\omega^2 y$

3 (a) (i) $z = \dfrac{9}{4}\cos 2x - \dfrac{x^7}{210} + \dfrac{k}{2}x^2 + cx + d$

(ii) $y = \dfrac{1}{x} - \dfrac{5}{6}x^3 + kx + c$

(iii) $y = \sin^3 x + k$

(b) Solving $2\frac{5}{6} = k + c$ and $11\frac{1}{6} = 2k + c$ gives

$k = 8\frac{1}{3}$ and $c = -5\frac{1}{2}$.

4 (a) $v = -36 + 24t - 3t^2$, so $v = 0$ when $t^2 - 8t + 12 = 0$ i.e. $t = 2$ or 6.

v is negative for $t < 2$ and $t > 6$ and it is positive for $2 < t < 6$. The particle therefore changes direction when $t = 2$ and 6.

(b) $a = 24 - 6t$, so the required accelerations are $a = 12$ and $a = -12$.

5 (a) (–1, –10), (–0.5, –9.28571), (0, –8.88799), (0.5, –8.88799), (1, –9.31258), (1.5, –10.1046) (2, –11.1603), (2.5, –12.3857), (3, –13.7175)

(b) (–1, 0), (–0.5, –1.66667), (0, –3.54167), (0.5, –3.54167), (1, –8.15705), (1.5, –9.12660) (2, –10.3508), (2.5, –11.7112), (3, –13.1461)

(c) (–1, –5), (–0.5, –2.5), (0, –7.5) (0.5, –7.5), (1, –8.05556), (1.5, –9.04457), (2, –10.2854), (2.5, –11.6580), (3, –13.1017)

Numerical solutions

1 (a)

t	x	u
0	20	15
0.5	30	−20
1	22.5	−30

After 1 second, $\frac{dx}{dt} = u + 5 \approx -25 \text{ ms}^{-1}$.

(b) $\frac{d}{dt}\left(\frac{dx}{dt} - 5\right) = -2x - 2\left(\frac{dx}{dt} - 5\right)$

$$\frac{d^2x}{dt^2} + 2\frac{dx}{dt} + 2x = 10$$

2 (a)

t	V	x
0	15	0
1	2.5	15
2	11.9	17.5
3	7.8	29.4
4	11.7	37.2
5	8.0	48.9

The values of V suggest the parachutist alternately slows down and accelerates, which is clearly not what really happens.

(b) $\int \frac{10 \, dV}{V^2 - 100} = \int -dt$

$$t = -\frac{10}{20} \ln\left(\frac{V-10}{V+10}\right) + C$$

Initially, $t = 0$ and $V = 15$, so

$$C = \frac{1}{2} \ln\left(\frac{1}{5}\right)$$

Then $\ln\left(\frac{5V-50}{V+10}\right) = -2t$

$\Rightarrow 5V - 50 = e^{-2t}(V + 10)$

$\Rightarrow V = \frac{10(5 + e^{-2t})}{(5 - e^{-2t})}$

As t becomes large, $e^{-2t} \to 0$ and $V \to 10$.

The exact solution at $t = 1$ is $V = 10.6$ so a time-step $dt = 1$, overshoots this with a large error. A much smaller time-step such as $dt = 0.2$ is necessary.

3 Let $V = \frac{dy}{dt}$, then

$$\frac{dV}{dt} = \frac{d^2y}{dt^2} = -\frac{120}{500}y - \frac{40}{500}\frac{dy}{dt}$$

$$\Rightarrow \frac{dV}{dt} = -0.08V - 0.24y$$

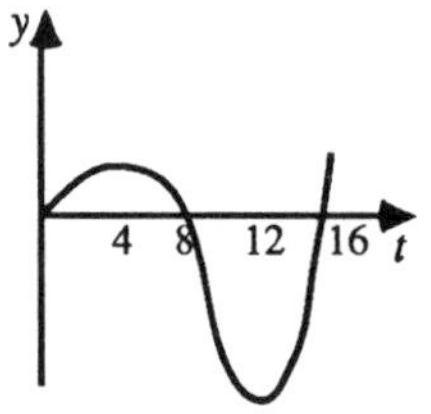

4 $p = q + r = 1 \Rightarrow \frac{dp}{dt} + \frac{dq}{dt} + \frac{dr}{dt} = 0$

$$\Rightarrow \frac{dq}{dt} = -\left(\frac{dp}{dt} + \frac{dr}{dt}\right) = 2p - q$$

t	p	q	r
0	1	0	0
0.2	0.60	0.40	0
0.4	0.36	0.56	0.08
0.6	0.22	0.59	0.19
0.8	0.13	0.56	0.31
1.0	0.08	0.50	0.42

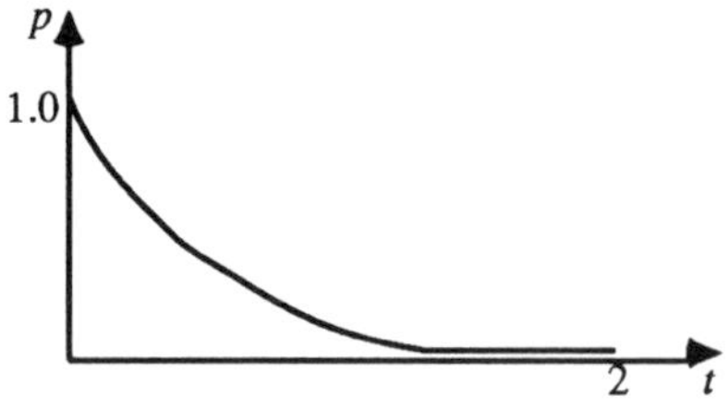

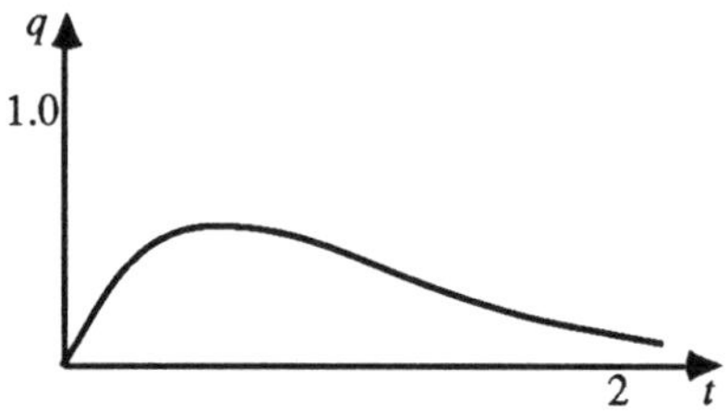

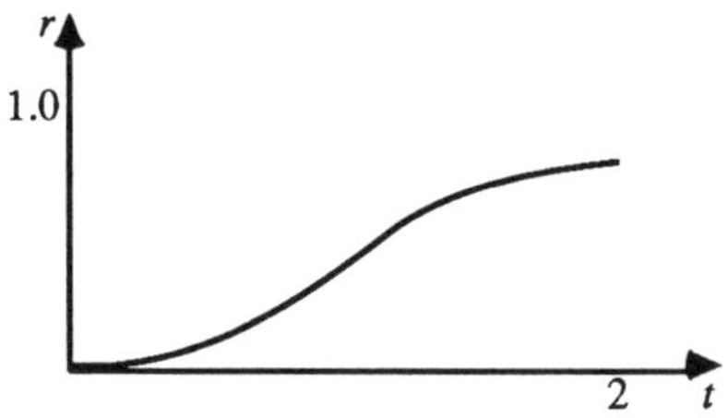

First order equations

1 (a) $\int \frac{1}{y^2} dy = \int 3 \, dx \Rightarrow -\frac{1}{y} = 3x + c$

$$\Rightarrow y = -\frac{1}{3x + c}$$

(b) $\int \frac{1}{y-4} dy = \int \frac{1}{x} dx \Rightarrow y = kx + 4$

2 $\int dy = \int \frac{x}{x^2 + 1} dx$

$$\Rightarrow y = \frac{1}{2} \ln | x^2 + 1 | + c$$

$$\Rightarrow y = \frac{1}{2} \ln \left| \frac{x^2 + 1}{2} \right|$$

3 $\int \frac{1}{4-v^2}\,dv = \int dt$

$\Rightarrow \frac{1}{4}(\ln|2+v| - \ln|2-v|) = t + c$

Using $v = 0$ and $t = 0$, $c = 0$.

So $\frac{2+v}{2-v} = e^{4t} \Rightarrow v = 2\frac{e^{4t}-1}{e^{4t}+1}$

4 (a) $v = \frac{1}{4} - \frac{1}{2}t - \frac{1}{2}t^2$

(b) $y = 0.1\sin 2t - 0.2\cos 2t$

(c) $y = te^{3t}$

5 (a) $y = Ke^{-(1/2)x} + 12$

(b) $v = Ke^{3x} - e^x$

6 $y = Ke^{-4x} + \frac{1}{2}x - \frac{3}{8}$

Using $(0, \frac{1}{2})$, $K = \frac{7}{8}$

$y = \frac{7}{8}e^{-4x} + \frac{1}{2}x - \frac{3}{8}$

7 $\int_0^y \frac{1}{\sqrt{(1-y^2)}}\,dy = \int_{\frac{\pi}{6}}^x dx$

$\Rightarrow \sin^{-1} y = x - \frac{\pi}{6}$

$\Rightarrow y = \sin\left(x - \frac{\pi}{6}\right)$

8 $\int_1^y dy = \int_{\frac{\pi}{4}}^{\theta} \frac{2}{1+\cos 2\theta}\,d\theta = \int_{\frac{\pi}{4}}^{\theta} \sec^2\theta\,d\theta$

$\Rightarrow y - 1 = \tan\theta - 1 \Rightarrow y = \tan\theta$

Second order equations

1 (a) CF $= (Ax+B)e^{-3x}$, PI $= 0$
$y = (Ax+B)e^{-3x}$

(b) CF $= e^{3x/2}\left(A\cos\left(\frac{\sqrt{3}x}{2}\right) + B\sin\left(\frac{\sqrt{3}x}{2}\right)\right)$, PI $= 0$

$y = e^{3x/2}\left(A\cos\left(\frac{\sqrt{3}x}{2}\right) + B\sin\left(\frac{\sqrt{3}x}{2}\right)\right)$

(c) CF $= Ae^{2t} + Be^{-t}$, PI $= -\frac{6}{5}\sin 2t + \frac{2}{5}\cos 2t$

$x = Ae^{2t} + Be^{-t} - \frac{6}{5}\sin 2t + \frac{2}{5}\cos 2t$

(d) CF $= Ae^{3x} + Be^{-2x}$, PI $= -xe^{-2x}$
$y = Ae^{3x} + Be^{-2x} - xe^{-2x}$

(e) CF $= (Ax+B)e^{-x}$, PI $= x^2 - 4x + 3$
$y = (Ax+B)e^{-x} + x^2 - 4x + 3$

2 $y = Ae^{3x} + Be^x + \frac{1}{2}xe^{3x}$

$\frac{dy}{dx} = 3Ae^{3x} + Be^x + \frac{3}{2}xe^{3x} + \frac{1}{2}e^{3x}$

Substituting initial conditions gives

$A = -\frac{3}{4}$ and $B = \frac{7}{4}$. So

$y = -\frac{3}{4}e^{3x} + \frac{7}{4}e^x + \frac{1}{2}xe^{3x}$

3 $x = Ae^{3t} + Be^{-(1/2)t}$

$\frac{dx}{dt} = 3Ae^{3t} - \frac{1}{2}Be^{-(1/2)t}$

Substituting initial conditions gives

$A = 2$ and $B = -2$

$x = 2e^{3t} - 2e^{-(1/2)t}$

4 $y = (Ax+B)e^{2x} - \frac{5}{13}\cos 3x - \frac{12}{13}\sin 3x$

$\frac{dy}{dx} = Ae^{2x} + 2(Ax+B)e^{2x} + \frac{15}{13}\sin 3x - \frac{36}{13}\cos 3x$

Substituting initial conditions gives

$B = \frac{18}{13}$ and $A = 0$. So

$y = \frac{18}{13}e^{2x} - \frac{5}{13}\cos 3x - \frac{12}{13}\sin 3x$

5 $\frac{dy}{dx} = \frac{dz}{dx} + 2x$, $\frac{d^2y}{dx^2} = \frac{d^2z}{dx^2} + 2$. So $\frac{d^2z}{dx^2} = -z$.

Hence $z = A\cos x + B\sin x$

and $y = A\cos x + B\sin x + x^2$

6 (a) $x = A\cos 2t + B\sin 2t$

$\frac{dx}{dt} = -2A\sin 2t + 2B\cos 2t$

Substituting gives $A = 3$ and $B = 0$, so $x = 3\cos 2t$.

(b) $x = Ae^{-4t} + Be^{-t} + \frac{1}{2}\sin t - \frac{1}{2}\cos t$

$\frac{dx}{dt} = -4Ae^{-4t} - Be^{-t} + \frac{1}{2}\cos t + \frac{1}{2}\sin t$

Substituting initial conditions gives

$A = -1$ and $B = \frac{9}{2}$. So

$x = \frac{9}{2}e^{-t} - e^{-4t} + \frac{1}{2}\sin t - \frac{1}{2}\cos t$

MISCELLANEOUS EXERCISES

MATHEMATICAL STRUCTURE

1 (a) and (c) are isomorphic groups.
(b) is not a group. $2 \times 2 = 0$ and so (b) is not closed.

2 $a * 0 = a + 0 - 0 = a$
$0 * a = 0 + a - 0 = a$

$*$ is **both** commutative and associative.

3 The isomorphism is given by

$$6 \leftrightarrow 1, 4 \leftrightarrow -1, 2 \leftrightarrow j \text{ or } -j, 8 \leftrightarrow -j \text{ or } j.$$

4 (a) $a \cup b$ (b) $a \cap b'$

5 (a) $[(a' \cap b) \cup a] \cap [b \cup (a \cap b')]$

(b) $a \cup b$

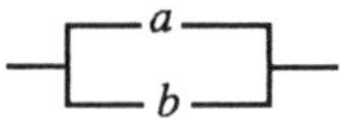

6 (a) $1 \sim \{1\}, 2 \sim \{2, 4, 3, 1\}, 3 \sim \{3, 4, 2, 1\}, 4 \sim \{4, 1\}$

(b) Yes. It is generated by both 2 and 3.

7 (a) $\text{RTRT}(x) = \text{RTR}(x + 1) = \ldots = x$, as required.

(b) RT^{10}R

8 (a) There is the identity element (order 1), three rotations of 180° (order 2) about the lines joining mid-points of opposite edges and eight rotations of 120° (order 3) – two fix point A, two fix B, etc.

(b) It is sufficient to observe the isomorphism with the group of symmetries of a rectangle.

(c) By Lagrange's theorem, all elements of such a subgroup must have orders 1, 2 or 4 and so can only be the identity element and three rotations of 180°.

For questions 9 to 11, having shown the statement is true for $n = 1$, the crucial relationships to demonstrate are:

10 $k(k + 1)! + ((k + 1)^2 + 1)(k + 1)! = (k + 1)(k + 2)!$

11 $5(2^k + 3M) - 2^{k+1} = 3(5M + 2^k)$

12 $\dfrac{k(3k + 5)}{4(k + 1)(k + 2)} + \dfrac{1}{(k + 1)(k + 3)} = \dfrac{(k + 1)(3k + 8)}{4(k + 2)(k + 3)}$

MATRICES

1 (a) $\begin{bmatrix} 1 & 2 \\ 0 & 1 \end{bmatrix}$

(b) A shear with the x-axis invariant and $(0, 1) \rightarrow (2, 1)$.

(c) $\mathbf{M}^{-1} = \begin{bmatrix} 1 & -2 \\ 0 & 1 \end{bmatrix}$

Shear with x-axis invariant and $(0, 1) \rightarrow (-2, 1)$.

2 (a) $\begin{bmatrix} 0.4 & 0.6 \\ 0.6 & 0.4 \end{bmatrix}$ (b) 0.52

(c) $\begin{bmatrix} 1 \\ 1 \end{bmatrix}$ (d) $\frac{1}{2}$

3 $\begin{bmatrix} -2 & 3 \\ 1 & 5 \end{bmatrix}^{-1} \begin{bmatrix} 0 \\ 13 \end{bmatrix} = \begin{bmatrix} 3 \\ 2 \end{bmatrix}$

4 $(5, 3, 0)$

5 (a) $1, \begin{bmatrix} 1 \\ 3 \end{bmatrix}$; $-1, \begin{bmatrix} -3 \\ 1 \end{bmatrix}$

(b) $R = \begin{bmatrix} 1 & -3 \\ 3 & 1 \end{bmatrix} \begin{bmatrix} 1 & 0 \\ 0 & -1 \end{bmatrix} \begin{bmatrix} 1 & -3 \\ 3 & 1 \end{bmatrix}^{-1} = \frac{1}{5} \begin{bmatrix} -4 & 3 \\ 3 & 4 \end{bmatrix}$

6 The planes are not parallel to each other and so it is sufficient to show that the equations have infinitely many solutions because 5 ① + ③ = 7②.

7 (a) $\begin{bmatrix} p & 0 \\ q & 1 \end{bmatrix} \begin{bmatrix} 0 \\ 1 \end{bmatrix} = \begin{bmatrix} 0 \\ 1 \end{bmatrix} \Rightarrow$ eigenvalue is 1.

$\begin{bmatrix} p & 0 \\ q & 1 \end{bmatrix} \begin{bmatrix} p - 1 \\ q \end{bmatrix} = p \begin{bmatrix} p - 1 \\ q \end{bmatrix} \Rightarrow$ eigenvalue is p.

(b) $\mathbf{T}^n = \begin{bmatrix} 0 & -1 \\ 1 & 1 \end{bmatrix} \begin{bmatrix} 1 & 0 \\ 0 & 1/2 \end{bmatrix}^n \begin{bmatrix} 0 & -1 \\ 1 & 1 \end{bmatrix}^{-1}$

$$= \begin{bmatrix} \left(\frac{1}{2}\right)^n & 0 \\ 1 - \left(\frac{1}{2}\right)^n & 1 \end{bmatrix}$$

8 $x_1 = 1.3,\ x_2 = -2.4,\ x_3 = 3.2$

9 $\begin{bmatrix} 1 & 0 & 0 \\ 1.5 & 1 & 0 \\ 0.5 & 0.2 & 1 \end{bmatrix} \begin{bmatrix} 2 & 1 & 1 \\ 0 & 2.5 & -0.5 \\ 0 & 0 & 1.6 \end{bmatrix} \begin{bmatrix} x_1 \\ x_2 \\ x_3 \end{bmatrix} = \begin{bmatrix} 6 \\ 17 \\ 3 \end{bmatrix}$

$x_1 = 2,\ x_2 = 3,\ x_3 = -1$

10 (a) $\left[\begin{array}{ccc|c} 1 & 0 & 2 & d+4 \\ 0 & 1 & -2 & -\frac{1}{2}(d+6) \\ 0 & 0 & c+6 & d+1 \end{array}\right]$

(b) $x = -2, y = 5, z = 5$

(c) (i) $d = -1$

(ii) $\begin{bmatrix} x \\ y \\ z \end{bmatrix} = \begin{bmatrix} 3 \\ -2.5 \\ 0 \end{bmatrix} + \lambda \begin{bmatrix} -2 \\ 2 \\ 1 \end{bmatrix}$

COMPLEX NUMBERS

1 (a) $r = 2, \theta = \dfrac{2\pi n}{3}, n = 0, 1, 2$

(b) $1, 5 \pm j$

2 $\dfrac{\sqrt{2}}{5}$, 98.1°

3 256

4 (a) Circle, centre (0, 4) radius 4.

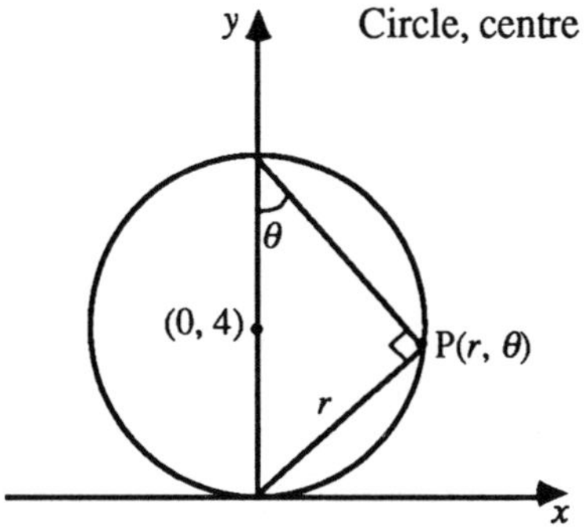

$r = 8 \sin \theta$

(b) $R = r^2 = 64 \sin^2 \theta = 32\,(1 - \cos 2\theta)$

$\phi = 2\theta \Rightarrow R = 32\,(1 - \cos \phi)$

(c) A cardioid.

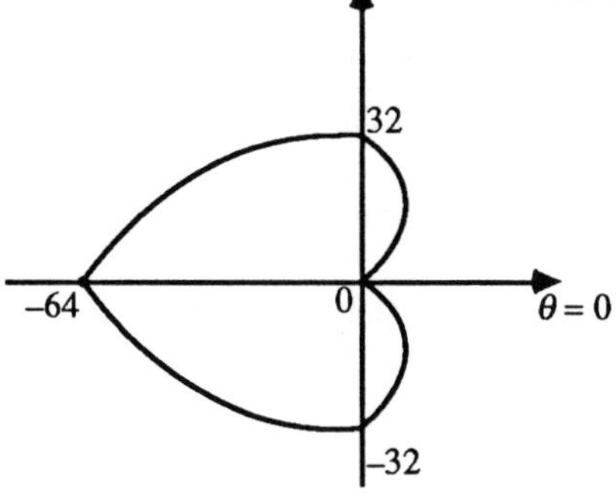

5 (a) A circle, centre $(5\frac{1}{2}, 0)$ and radius $1\frac{1}{2}$.

(b) $\sqrt{3} + j = [2, \frac{\pi}{6}]$ and so the mapping is an enlargement scale factor 2 and an anti-clockwise rotation of $\frac{\pi}{6}$.

Hence the image is a circle centre $\left(\frac{11\sqrt{3}}{2}, \frac{11}{2}\right)$ and radius 3.

6 The mapping represents an anti-clockwise rotation, followed by an enlargement scale factor $\frac{1}{2}$ and a translation through $\begin{bmatrix} 0 \\ -1 \end{bmatrix}$.

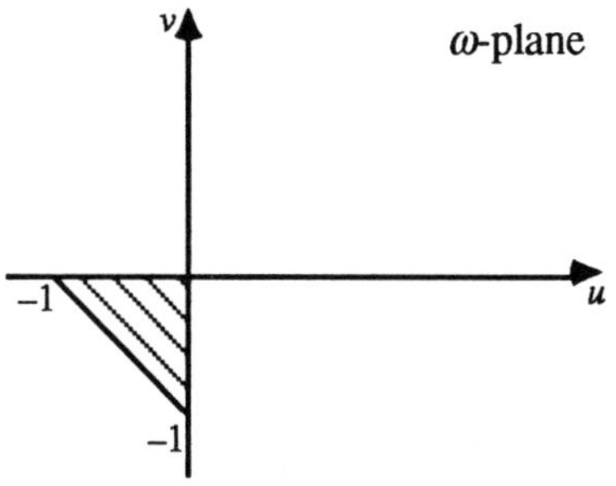

7 $2\cos^2 z - 1 = 2 \times \frac{1}{4}(e^{2jz} + 2 + e^{-2jz}) - 1$

$= \frac{1}{2}(e^{2jz} + e^{-2jz})$

$= \cos 2z$

8 $8 \to \frac{1}{8}, 6j \to -\frac{1}{6}j$

Since circles through the origin map onto a straight line under an inversion, the image is the straight line through $-\frac{1}{6}j$ and $\frac{1}{8}$.

9 $\dfrac{3z-1}{z+3} = \dfrac{3(z+3)-10}{z+3} = 3 - \dfrac{10}{z+3}$

Translation $\begin{bmatrix} 3 \\ 0 \end{bmatrix}$, inversion, enlargement × 10, rotation of 180° about origin, translation of $\begin{bmatrix} 3 \\ 0 \end{bmatrix}$.

10 $z^2 - z + 1 = 0 \Rightarrow z = \dfrac{1 \pm j\sqrt{3}}{2}$

11 $z_0 = j, z_1 = j - aj, z_2 = j - a(j - aj)$

Then $z_2 = z_0 \Rightarrow a = 0$ (period 1) or $a = 1$ (period 2).

12 (a) $j - \dfrac{j}{z+1}$

(b) A translation of $\begin{bmatrix} 1 \\ 0 \end{bmatrix}$, inversion, rotation of 270° and translation of $\begin{bmatrix} 0 \\ 1 \end{bmatrix}$ produce the circle:

$$|z - \tfrac{5}{3}j| = \tfrac{1}{3}$$

NUMERICAL METHODS

1 2% (one third of 6%)

2 (a) Second order, since doubling the number of strips divides the error by 2^2.

(b) Trapezium or mid-ordinate rule

3 $h = \frac{2-1}{4} = 0.25$

$\frac{1}{12}$ [log 1 + log 2 + 4(log 1.25 + log 1.75) + 2 log 1.5]

= 0.16775

4 $h = \frac{\pi}{12}$. Mean value = $\frac{2}{\pi} \times 1.18731 \approx 0.75587$.

5 $g'(x) = -2(1+2x)^{-2}$, $g''(x) = 8(1+2x)^{-3}$

$\Rightarrow g(1+h) \approx \frac{1}{3} - \frac{2}{9}h + \frac{4}{27}h^2$

$\Rightarrow g(x) \approx \frac{1}{3} - \frac{2}{9}(x-1) + \frac{4}{27}(x-1)^2$

$\approx \frac{1}{27}(19 - 14x + 4x^2)$

6 $C'(x) = -\sin x$, $C''(x) = -\cos x$. $c(0) = 1$, $c'(0) = -1$, $c''(0) = -1$. So $C(x) \approx 1 - \frac{1}{2}x^2$.

Absolute errors:

	C(x)	c(x)	| c(x – C(x) |
x = 0.5	0.87758	0.875	0.00258
x = 1.0	0.54030	0.5	0.04030
x = 1.25	0.31532	0.21875	0.09657
x = 1.5	0.07074	–0.125	0.19574
x = 2.0	–0.41615	–1.00000	0.56385

7 $\frac{4}{5} - \frac{4}{25}x + \frac{4}{125}x^2 - \frac{4}{625}x^3 + \frac{4}{3125}x^4 + \ldots$

for $-5 < x < 5$.

$\frac{4}{5+\frac{1}{5}} \approx \frac{4}{5} - \frac{4}{125} + \frac{4}{3125} - \frac{4}{78125} + \frac{4}{1953125}$

= 0.7692308

Then $\frac{4}{13} \approx \frac{2}{5} \times 0.7692308 \approx 0.30769$

$x = 8$ lies outside the radius of convergence. (Try using $x = 8$ and see what happens!)

8 (a) Sign changes indicate roots:

$f(-2) = -2$, $f(-1) = +1$, $f(0) = -2$,
$f(2) = -2$, $f(3) = +13$

(b) $4x = x^3 - 2$, $x = \frac{x^3}{4} - 0.5$

$x = -0.54$

(c) Formula (b) $g'(2.21) = 3.68$ (greater than 1)

Formula (c) $g'(2.21) = 0.27$ (less than 1)

9 (a) [3, 4]

(b) 3.6180

(c) $f(-1) = 0$, so $(x+1)$ is a factor.

$(x+1)(x^2 - 5x + 5) = 0$

$x = -1, \ \frac{1}{2}(5 \pm \sqrt{5})$

10 Runge Kutta has fourth order of accuracy, so doubling the number of strips will divide the error by 2^4.

If v is the correct value,

$16.4902 - v = 16(16.4552 - v)$
$v = 16.453$ (to 3 d.p.)

DIFFERENTIAL EQUATIONS

1 (a) $\frac{d^2x}{dt^2} = 100e^{-t-2}$

(b) $x = 100e^{-t-2} + At + B$, where A, B are constants.

(c) As time increases, the exponential term in the solution will tend to zero and the particle will tend towards a constant velocity.

(d) $x = 100e^{-t-2} + 250t - 100e^{-2}$

2 (a)

x	y	dy/dx	dx	dy
0	5	0	0.5	0
0.5	5	0.549409	0.5	0.274704
1	5.274704	2.992485	0.5	1.496242
1.5	6.770947	–1.040822	0.5	–0.520411
2	6.250536	–1.676493	0.5	–0.838246

(b) The exact integral is $y = -\cos(1.5^2 x) + c$, where $c = 6$. Therefore the exact solution is $y = 5.0398$ (to 4 d.p.).

(c) Percentage error = 24.0% (to 3 s.f.)

3 $dq = 0.2i$, $di = -i - 0.8q$

i	q	t
0	3	0
–2.4	3	0.2
–2.4	2.52	0.4
–2.016	2.04	0.6
–1.632	1.6368	0.8
–1.30944	1.3104	1

4 (a) $\int \frac{\mathrm{d}y}{y} = \int x(2 \ln x + 1)\,\mathrm{d}x$

$\ln y = x^2 \ln x + c$

$y = Ae^{x^2 \ln x}$

(b) $y = e^{x^2 \ln x}$

5 $y = Ae^{-2x} + \frac{1}{4} e^{2x}$

$y = \frac{1}{4}(e^{2x} - e^{-2x})$

6 $y = Ae^{2x} + \frac{1}{5} \sin 4x - \frac{1}{10} \cos 4x$

$y = \frac{1}{10} e^{2x} + \frac{1}{5} \sin 4x - \frac{1}{10} \cos 4x$

7 (a) –

(b) $x = Ae^{-3t} + Be^{-5t} + 0.7 \sin t - 0.4 \cos t$

(c) $x = 0.404$ metres

8 $x = (0.2 - t)e^{-t} + 0.6 \sin 2t - 0.2 \cos 2t$

9 $q = e^{-t} (\cos t + 2 \sin t) - \cos 2t - \frac{1}{2} \sin 2t$

$\frac{\mathrm{d}q}{\mathrm{d}t} = e^{-t} (\cos t - 3 \sin t) + 2 \sin 2t - \cos 2t$

10 (a) $\frac{\mathrm{d}u}{\mathrm{d}t} = 0 \Rightarrow u = c$

$\frac{\mathrm{d}v}{\mathrm{d}t} = \frac{\mathrm{d}x}{\mathrm{d}t} - \frac{\mathrm{d}y}{\mathrm{d}t} = 2(x - y) = 2v$

$\Rightarrow v = Ae^{2t}$

(b) $x + y = 100$

$x - y = 20\, e^{2t}$

$\Rightarrow x = 50 + 10e^{2t}$

$y = 50 - 10e^{2t}$

INDEX